COUNTER-CURRENTS

COUNTER-CURRENTS

BY

AGNES REPPLIER, *1855 - 1950*

Essay Index Reprint Series

BOOKS FOR LIBRARIES PRESS
FREEPORT, NEW YORK

PS
2696
.C7
1971

INTERNATIONAL STANDARD BOOK NUMBER:
0-8369-2026-0

LIBRARY OF CONGRESS CATALOG CARD NUMBER:
73-121504

PRINTED IN THE UNITED STATES OF AMERICA

Note

(TO THE ORIGINAL EDITION)

THESE nine essays, in their original form, were published in the *Atlantic Monthly* during the past three years.

Contents

COUNTER-CURRENTS

The Cost of Modern Sentiment

WE are rising dizzily and fearlessly on the crest of a great wave of sentiment. When the wave breaks, we may find ourselves submerged, and in danger of drowning; but for the present we are full of hope and high resolve. Forty years ago we stood in shallow water, and mocked at the mid-Victorian sentiment, then ebbing slowly with the tide. We have nothing now in common with that fine, thin, tenacious conception of life and its responsibilities. We do not prate about valour for men, and domesticity for women. A vague humanity is our theme. We do not feel the fastidious distaste for repulsive details which made our grandparents culpably negligent. All knowledge, apart from its quality, and apart from our requirements, now seems to us desirable. Taste is no longer a controlling force. We do not, if we can help it, look "that jade, Duty," — I use Sir Walter Scott's phrase, and he knew the lady in question better than do most men, — squarely in the face; but we speak well of her behind her back, which is more than Sir Walter did. To hear us talk, one would imagine that she never cost a pang.

The sentiment of to-day is social and philanthropic. It has no affiliations with art, which stands aloof from it, — a new experience for the world. It dominates periodical literature, minor fiction, and serious verse; but it has so far given nothing of permanent value to letters. It is in high favour with politicians, and is echoed loudly from all party platforms. It has unduly influenced our attitude toward the war in Europe, and toward our

defences at home. It is a force to be reckoned with, and to be controlled. It is
capable of raising us to a better and
clearer vision, or of weakening our judgment and shattering our common sense.
If we value our safety, we must forever
bear in mind that sentiment is subjec-
tive, and a personal thing. However exalted and however ardent, it cannot be
accepted as a scale for justice, or as a
test for truth.

The issues with which our modern
sentiment chiefly concerns itself are the
conditions of labour, the progress of women, the social evil, and — for the past
two years — the overwhelming question
of peace and war. Sometimes these issues
are commingled. Always they have a
bearing upon one another. There is also
a distinct and perilous tendency toward
sentiment in matters political and judi-
cial; while an excess of emotionalism is
the stumbling-block of those noble associations which work for the protection of

animals. It is profoundly discouraging to read in the accredited organ of an American humane society an angry protest against Vilhjalmur Stefansson's being permitted the use of Eskimo dogs on his Arctic explorations, because, forsooth, when he went hungry, the dogs went hungry too, and because their feet were hurt by the ice. The writer (a woman) reminds us that these dogs (like all other animals) are not "free agents"; and she calls upon public opinion and law to rescue them. We hear about the "long arm of the law," but it would be a giant stretch that could reach Stefansson in his icefields. "Men who do such things," she affirms, "are not heroes of the highest type; and, anyway, when you have found or explored the North Pole or the South Pole, what can you do with it?"

This query is hard to answer. Perhaps no explorer wants to do anything with the Poles; but just leave them as they are, uncolonized for the present. They

Cost of Modern Sentiment

are not the only things in the world which have no commercial value. But if Stefansson is not a hero, of what stuff are heroes made, and where shall we look to find one? And with all Europe crying out in its agony of pain, is it worth our while to worry over a few dogs, who are doing, under hard conditions, the work they are fitted to do?

The same journal insults the intelligence of its readers by printing a wild rhapsody of Mrs. Annie Besant's, apparently under the illusion that it can be accepted as an argument for vegetarianism. I venture to quote one particularly mad paragraph as an illustration of the unplumbed depths to which emotional humanitarianism can descend:—

"The killing of animals in order to devour their flesh is so obviously an outrage on all humane feelings, that one is almost ashamed to mention it in a paper that is regarding man as a director of evolution. If any one who eats flesh could

5

Counter-Currents

be taken to the shambles, to watch the agonized struggles of the terrified victims as they are dragged to the spot where knife or mallet slays them; if he could be made to stand with the odours of the blood reeking in his nostrils; if there his astral vision could be opened so that he might see the filthy creatures that flock round to feast on the loathsome exhalations, and see also the fear and horror of the slaughtered beasts as they arrive in the astral world, and send back thence currents of dread and hatred that flow between men and animals in constantly refed streams; if a man could pass through these experiences, he would 'be cured of meat-eating forever."

Now, when one has belonged for many years to the society which printed this precious paragraph, when one has believed all one's life that to be sentient is to possess rights, and that, not kindness only, but justice to the brute creation is an essential element of decent living, it

6

Cost of Modern Sentiment

is hard to be confronted with unutterable nonsense about astral currents and astral visions. It is harder still to be held indirectly responsible for the publication of such nonsense, and to entertain for the thousandth time the weary conviction that common sense is not a determining factor in humanity.

Mr. Chesterton, upon whom the delight of startling his readers never seems to pall, has declared that men are more sentimental than women, "whose only fault is their excessive sense." Also that the apparent absorption of the modern world in social service is not the comprehensive thing it seems. The general public still remains indifferent. This may or may not be true. It is as hard for Mr. Chesterton as for the rest of us to know much about that remnant of the public which is not writing, or lecturing, or collecting data, or collecting funds, or working for clubs and societies. But no one can say that the social reformer is the slighted creature that he was a half-century ago. He meets with the most distinguished consideration, and he is always accorded the first hearing in print and on the platform. He commands our respect when he deals soberly with sober facts in sober language, when his conclusions are just, his statements irrefutable. He is less praiseworthy when he flies to fiction, an agreeable but unconvincing medium; or to verse, which, as the theologian said of " Paradise Lost," "proves nothing." It is very good verse sometimes, and its grace of sentiment, its note of appeal, find an easy echo in the reader's heart.

A little poem called " The Factories," published in "McClure's Magazine" for September, 1912, gives an almost perfect example of the modern point of view, of the emotional treatment of an economic question, and of the mental confusion which arises from the substitution of sympathy for exactness.

Cost of Modern Sentiment

"I have shut my little sister in from life and light
   (For a rose, for a ribbon, for a wreath across my
      hair),
I have made her restless feet still until the night,
   Locked from sweets of summer, and from wild
      spring air:
I who ranged the meadow-lands, free from sun to
      sun,
   Free to sing, and pull the buds, and watch the
      far wings fly,
I have bound my sister till her playing-time is
      done, —
   Oh, my little sister, was it I? — was it I?

"I have robbed my sister of her day of maiden-
      hood
   (For a robe, for a feather, for a trinket's restless
      spark),
Shut from Love till dusk shall fall, how shall she
      know good,
   How shall she pass scatheless through the sin-
      lit dark?
I who could be innocent, I who could be gay,
   I who could have love and mirth before the
      light went by,
I have put my sister in her mating-time away, —
   Sister, my young sister, was it I? — was it I?

"I have robbed my sister of the lips against her
      breast

9

Counter-Currents

(For a coin, for the weaving of my children's
  lace and lawn),
Feet that pace beside the loom, hands that can-
  not rest:
  How can she know motherhood, whose strength
    is gone?
I who took no heed of her, starved and labor
  worn,
  I against whose placid heart my sleepy gold-
    heads lie,
Round my path they cry to me, little souls un-
  born, —
  God of Life — Creator! It was I! It was I."

Now if by "I" is meant the average
woman who wears the "robe," the "ribbon," the "feather," and possibly —
though rarely — the "wreath across my
hair," "I" must protest distinctly against
assuming a guilt which is none of mine.
I have not shut my little sister in a factory, any more than I have ranged the
meadow-lands, "free from sun to sun."
What I probably am doing is trying to
persuade my sister to cook my dinner,
and sweep my house, and help me to
take care of my "gold-heads," who are

not always so sleepy as I could desire. If my sister declines to do this at a wage equal to her factory earnings, and with board and lodging included, she is well within her rights, and I have no business, as is sometimes my habit, weakly to complain of her decision. If I made my household arrangements acceptable to her, she would come. As this is difficult or distasteful to me, she goes to a factory instead. The right of every man and woman to do the work he or she chooses to do, and can do, at what wages, and under what conditions he or she can command, is the fruit of centuries of struggle. It is now so well established that only the trade unions venture to deny it.

In that vivid and sad study of New York factory life, published some years ago by the Century Company, under the title of "The Long Day," a girl who is out of work, and who has lost her few possessions in a lodging-house fire, seeks counsel of a wealthy stranger who has befriended her.

"The lady looked at me a moment out of fine, clear eyes.

"'You would not go into service, I suppose?' she asked slowly.

"I had never thought of such an alternative before, but I met it without a moment's hesitation. 'No, I would not care to go into service,' I replied; and, as I did so, the lady's face showed mingled disappointment and disgust.

"'That is too bad,' she answered, 'for, in that case, I'm afraid I can do nothing for you.' And she went out of the room, leaving me, I must confess, not sorry for having thus bluntly decided against wearing the definite badge of servitude."

Here at least is a refreshingly plain statement of facts. The girl in question bore the servitude imposed upon her by the foremen of half a dozen factories; she slept for many months in quarters which no domestic servant would consent to occupy; she ate food which no servant would be asked to eat; she associated with young women whom no servant would accept as equals and companions. But, as she had voluntarily relinquished comfort, protection, and the grace of human relations between employer and employed, she accepted her chosen conditions, and tried successfully to better them along her chosen lines. The reader is made to understand that it was as unreasonable for the benevolent lady — who had visions of a trim and white-capped parlor-maid dancing before her eyes — to show "disappointment and disgust" because her overtures were rejected, as it would have been to charge the same lady with robbing the girl of her "day of maidenhood," and her "little souls unborn," by shutting her up in a factory. If we will blow our minds clear of generous illusions, we shall understand that an emotional verdict has no validity when offered as a criterion of facts.

Counter-Currents

The excess of sentiment, which is misleading in philanthropy and economics, grows acutely dangerous when it interferes with legislation, or with the ordinary rulings of morality. The substitution of a sentimental principle of authority for the impersonal processes of law confuses our understanding, and undermines our sense of justice. It is a painful truth that most laws have had their origin in a profound mistrust of human nature (even Mr. Olney admits that the Constitution, although framed in the interests of freedom, is not strictly altruistic); but the time is hardly ripe for brushing aside this ungenerous mistrust, and establishing the social order on a basis of pure enthusiasm. The reformers who light-heartedly announce that people are "tired of the old Constitution anyway," voice the buoyant creed of ignorance. I once heard a popular lecturer say of a popular idol that he "preferred making precedents to following them," and the

Cost of Modern Sentiment

remark evoked a storm of applause. It was plain that the audience considered following a precedent to be a timorous and unworthy thing for a strong man to do; and it was equally plain that nobody had given the matter the benefit of a serious thought. Believers in political faith-healing enjoy a supreme immunity from doubt.

This growing contempt for paltry but not unuseful restrictions, this excess of sentiment, combined with paucity of humour and a melodramatic attitude toward crime, has had some discouraging results. It is ill putting the strong man, or the avenging angel, or the sinned-against woman above the law, which is a sacred trust for the preservation of life and liberty. It is ill so to soften our hearts with a psychological interest in the lawbreaker that no criminal is safe from popularity. The "Nation" performed a well-timed duty when it commented grimly on the message sent to the public

Counter-Currents

by a murderer, and a singularly cold-blooded murderer, through the minister who attended him on the scaffold : " Mr. Beattie desired to thank his many friends for kind letters and expressions of interest, and the public for whatever sympathy was felt or expressed."

It sounds like a cabinet minister who has lost an honoured and beloved wife; not like an assassin who has lured *his* wife to a lonely spot, and there pitilessly killed her. One fails to see why " kind letters" and "expressions of interest" should have poured in upon this male-factor, just as one fails to see why a young woman who shot her lover a few months later in Columbus, Ohio, should have received an ovation in the court-room. It was not even her first lover (it seldom is); but when a gallant jury had acquitted her of all blame in the trifling matter of manslaughter, "the crowd shouted its approval"; "scores of women rushed up to her, and insisted upon kissing her";

16

Cost of Modern Sentiment

and an intrepid suitor, stimulated by circumstances which might have daunted a less mettlesome man, announced his intention of marrying the heroine on the spot.

In New York a woman murdered her lover because he refused his aid — a dastardly refusal — when her husband had cast her off. She was not only acquitted by a jury, — which was to be expected; but the husband, pleased with the turn affairs had taken, restored her to his home and his affections; and a sympathetic newspaper offered this explanation to a highly gratified public: "They are Sicilians, and in Sicily a woman may retrieve her own honour and avenge her husband's, only by doing as this woman had done."

Perhaps. But New York is not Sicily, our civilization is not Sicilian civilization, and our courts of law are not modelled on a Sicilian vendetta. The reporter described with all the eloquence of his craft

17

the young wife reconciled and joyous in her husband's arms, laughing and singing to her baby, happier than she had been at any time since her honeymoon. A pretty picture, if the shadow of a murdered man did not intrude upon it.

Our revolt from the old callous cruelty — the heart-sickening cruelty of the eighteenth century — has made us tender to criminals, and strangely lenient to their derelictions. It inspires genial visitors at Sing Sing to write about the "fine type" of men, sentenced for the foulest of crimes. It fills us all with concern lest detention prove irksome to the detained, lest baseball and well-appointed vaudeville should not sufficiently beguile the tedium of their leisure hours.

> "Imprisonment alone is not
> A thing of which we would complain,
> And ill-conwenience is our lot,
> But do not give the convick pain."

Sentiment has been defined as a revolt from the despotism of facts. It is often a revolt from authority, which, to the sentimentalist, seems forever despotic; and this revolt, or rather this easy disregard of authority, is fatal to the noblest efforts of the humanitarian. The women of wealth and position who from time to time fling themselves with ardour into the cause of striking shirt-waist-makers and garment-makers are always well intentioned, but not always well advised. In so far as they uphold the strikers in what are often just and reasonable demands, they do good work; and the substantial aid they give is sweetened by the spirit in which it is given, — the sense of fellow feeling with their kind. But there is no doubt that one of the lessons taught at such times to our foreign-born population is that the laws of our country may be disregarded with impunity. The picketers who attack the "scab" workers, and are arrested for disorderly conduct, are swiftly released, to become the heroines of the hour. I once remonstrated with a friend who had given bail for a dozen of these young lawbreakers, and she answered reproachfully: "But they are so ignorant and helpless. There were two poor bewildered girls in court yesterday who did not know enough English to understand the charge made against them. You could not conceive of anything more pathetic."

I said that a young woman who bowled over another young woman into the gutter understood perfectly the charge made against her, whether she spoke English or not. One does not have to study French or Spanish to know that one may not knock down a Frenchman or a Spaniard. No civilized country permits this robust line of argument. But reason is powerless when sentiment takes the helm. It would be as easy to argue with a conflagration as with unbalanced zeal. The vision of a good cause debauched by intemperance is familiar to all students of sociology; but it is no less melancholy for being both recognizable and ridiculous.

Cost of Modern Sentiment

A moderate knowledge of history —
which, though discouraging, is also enlightening — might prove serviceable to
all the enthusiasts who are engaged in
making over the world. Many of them
(in this country, at least) talk and write
as if nothing in particular had happened
between the Deluge and the Civil War.
That they sometimes know as little of
the Civil War as of the Deluge is proven
by the lament of an ardent and oratorical
pacifist that this great struggle should be
spoken of in school histories as a war for
the preservation of the Union, instead of
a war for the abolishment of slavery. A
lady lecturer, very prominent in social
work, has made the gratifying announcement that "the greatest discovery of the
nineteenth century is woman's discovery
of herself. It is only within the last fifty
years that it has come to be realized that
a woman is human, and has a right to
think and act for herself."

Now, after all, the past cannot be a

closed page, even to one so exclusively concerned with the present. A little less talking, a little more reading, and such baseless generalizations would be impossible, even on that stronghold of ignorance, the platform. If women failed to discover themselves a hundred, or five hundred years ago, it was because they had never been lost; it was because their important activities left them no leisure for self-contemplation. Yet Miss Jane Addams, who has toiled so long and so nobly for the bettering of social conditions, and whose work lends weight to her words, displays in "A New Conscience and an Ancient Evil" the same placid indifference to all that history has to tell. What can we say or think when confronted by such an astounding passage as this?

"Formerly all that the best woman possessed was a negative chastity, which had been carefully guarded by her parents and duennas. The chastity of the

Cost of Modern Sentiment

modern woman of self-directed activity
and of a varied circle of interests, which
give her an acquaintance with many men
as well as women, has therefore a new
value and importance in the establishment of social standards."

"Negative chastity!" "Parents and
duennas!" Was there ever such a maiden
outlook upon life! It was the chastity of
the married woman upon which rested
the security of the civilized world;—
that chastity which all men prized, and
most men assailed, which was preserved
in the midst of temptations unknown in
our decorous age, and held inviolate by
women whose "acquaintance with many
men" was at least as intimate and potent as anything experienced to-day.
Committees and congresses are not the
only meeting-grounds for the sexes.
"Remember," says M. Taine, writing of
a time which was not so long ago that
it need be forgotten, "remember that
during all these years women were par-

amount. They set the social tone, led society, and thereby guided public opinion.
When they appeared in the vanguard of
political progress, we may be sure that
the men were following."

We might be sure of the same thing
to-day, were it not for the tendency of
the modern woman to sever her rights
and wrongs from the rights and wrongs
of men ; thereby resembling the dispu-
tant who, being content to receive half
the severed baby, was adjudged by the
wise Solomon to be unworthy of any
baby at all. Half a baby is every whit as
valuable as the half-measure of reform
which fails to take into impartial consideration the inseparable claims of men
and women. Even in that most vital of
all reforms, the crusade against social
evils, the welfare of both sexes unifies the
subject. Here again we are swayed by
our anger at the indifference of an earlier
generation, at the hard and healthy attitude of men like Huxley, who had not

Cost of Modern Sentiment

imagination enough to identify the possible saint with the certain sinner, and who habitually confined their labours to fields which promised sure results. "In my judgment," wrote Huxley, "a domestic servant, who is perhaps giving half her wages to support her old parents, is more worthy of help than half a dozen Magdalens."

If we are forced to choose between them, — yes. But our esteem for the servant's self-respecting life, with its decent restraints and its purely normal activities, need not necessarily harden our hearts against the women whom Mr. Huxley called " Magdalens," nor against those whom we luridly designate as "white slaves." No work under Heaven is more imperative than the rescue of young and innocent girls; no crime is more dastardly than the sale of their youth and innocence; no charity is greater than that which lifts the sinner from her sin. But the fact that we habit-

Counter-Currents

ually apply the term "white slave" to the wilful prostitute as well as to the entrapped child shows that a powerful and popular sentiment is absolved from the shackles of accuracy. Also that this absolution confuses the minds of men. The sentimentalist pities the prostitute as a victim; the sociologist abhors her as a menace. The sentimentalist conceives that men prey, and women are preyed upon; the sociologist, aware that evil men and women prey upon one another ceaselessly and ravenously, has no measure of mercy for sin. The sentimentalist clings tenaciously to the association of youth with innocence; the sociologist knows that even the age-limit which the law fixes as a boundary-line of innocence has no corresponding restriction in fact. It is inconceivable that so many books and pamphlets dealing with this subject — books and pamphlets now to be found on every library shelf, and in the hands of young and old — should dare to ignore

26

Cost of Modern Sentiment

the balance of depravity, the swaying of the pendulum of vice.

A new and painful instance of the cost of modern sentiment is afforded by the statement of Miss Addams and other pacifists that middle-aged men are in favour of strengthened defences, and that young men oppose them, as savouring of militarism; that middle-aged men cling to the belief that war may be just and righteous, and that young men reject it, as unreservedly and inevitably evil. I am loath to accept this statement, as I am loath to accept all unpleasant statements; but if it be — as I presume it is — based upon data, or upon careful observation, it fits closely with my argument. The men under thirty are the men who have done their thinking in an era of undiluted sentiment. The men over forty were trained in a simpler, sterner creed. The call to duty embraced for them the call to arms.

"A country's a thing men should die for at need."

Counter-Currents

Some of them remember the days when Americans died for their country, and it is a recollection good for the soul. Again, the men over forty were taught by men; the men under thirty were taught by women; and the most dangerous economy practised by our extravagant Republic is the eliminating of the male teacher from our public schools. It is no insult to femininity to say that the feminization of boys is not a desirable development.

It was thought and said a few years ago that the substitution of organized charities for the somewhat haphazard benevolence of our youth would exclude sentiment, just as it excluded human and personal relations with the poor. It was thought and said that the steady advance of women in commercial and civic life would correct the sentimental bias which only Mr. Chesterton has failed to observe in the sex. No one who reads books and newspapers, or listens to speeches, or in-

Cost of Modern Sentiment

dulges in the pleasures of conversation can any longer cherish these illusions. No one can fail to see that sentiment is the motor power which drives us to intemperate words and actions; which weakens our judgment, and destroys our sense of proportion. The current phraseology, the current criticisms, the current enthusiasms of the day, all betray an excess of emotionalism. I pick up a table of statistics, furnishing economic data, and this is what I read: "Case 3. Two children under five. Mother shortly expecting the supreme trial of womanhood." That is the way to write stories, and, possibly, sermons; but it is not the way to write reports. I pick up a newspaper, and learn that an Englishman visiting the United States has made the interesting announcement that he is a reincarnation of one of the Pharaohs, and that an attentive and credulous band of disciples are gathering wisdom from his lips. I pick up a very serious and very

Counter-Currents

well-written book on the Brontë sisters, and am told that if I would "touch the very heart of the mystery that was Charlotte Brontë" (I had never been aware that there was anything mysterious about this famous lady), I will find it — save the mark! — in her passionate love for children.

"We are face to face here, not with a want, but with an abyss, depth beyond depth of tenderness, and longing, and frustration; with a passion that found no clear voice in her works because it was one with the elemental nature in her, undefined, unuttered, unutterable!"

It was certainly unuttered. It was not even hinted at in Miss Brontë's novels, nor in her voluminous correspondence. Her attitude toward children — so far as it found expression — was the arid but pardonable attitude of one who had been their reluctant caretaker and teacher. If, as we are now told, "there were moments when it was pain for Charlotte to

see the children born of and possessed
by other women," there were certainly
hours — so much she. makes clear to us
— in which the business of looking after
them wearied her beyond her powers of
endurance. It is true that Miss Brontë
said a few, a very few friendly words
about these little people. She did not,
like Swift, propose that babies should
be cooked and eaten. But this temperate regard, this restricted benevolence,
gives us no excuse for wallowing in
sentiment at her expense.

"If some virtues are new, all vices are
old." We can reckon the cost of misdi-
rected emotions by the price which the
past has paid for them. We know the
full significance of that irresponsible
sympathy which grows hysterical over
animals it should soberly protect; which
accuses the consumer of strange cruelties
to the producer; which condones law-
breaking and vindicates the lawbreaker;
which admits no difference between at-

tack and resistance, between a war of aggression and a war of defence; which confuses moral issues, ignores experience, and insults the intelligence of mankind.

The reformer whose heart is in the right place, but whose head is elsewhere, represents a waste of force; and we cannot afford any waste in the conservation of honour and goodness. We cannot afford errors of judgment, or errors of taste. The business of leading lives morally worthy of men is neither simple nor easy. And there are moments when, with the ageing Fontenelle, we sigh and say, "I am beginning to see things as they are. It is surely time for me to die."

Our Loss of Nerve

IF any lover of Hogarth will look at the series of pictures which tell the story of the Idle and the Industrious Apprentice, he will feel that while the industrious apprentice fitted admirably into his time and place, the idle apprentice had the misfortune to be born out of date. In what a different spirit would his tragic tale be told to-day, and what different emotions it would awaken. A poor tired boy, who ought to be at school or at play, sleeping for very exhaustion at his loom. A cruel boss daring to strike the worn-out lad. No better playground given him in the scant leisure which Sunday brings than a loathsome graveyard. No healthier sport provided for him than gaming. And, in the end, a lack of living wage forcing him to steal. Unhappy apprentice, to have lived and

sinned nearly two centuries too soon!
And as if this were not a fate bitter
enough for tears, he must needs have
contrasted with him at every step an industrious companion, whom that unen-
lightened age permitted to work as hard
as he pleased, even for the benefit of a
master, and to build up his own fortunes
on the foundation of his own worth. Hogarth's simple conception of personal responsibility and of personal equation is
as obsolete as the clumsy looms at which
his apprentices sit, and the full-skirted
coats they wear.

Yet the softening of the hard old rules,
the rigid old standards, has not tended
to strengthen the fibre of our race. Nobody supposes that the industrious apprentice had an enjoyable boyhood. As
far as we can see, going to church was
his sole recreation, as it was probably
the principal recreation of his master's
daughter, whose hymn-book he shares,
and whom he duly marries. *Her* home-

Our Loss of Nerve

life doubtless bore a strong resemblance
to the home-life of the tumultuous heroine of "Fanny's First Play," who tells us
with a heaving breast that she never knew
what a glorious thing life was until she
had knocked out a policeman's tooth.
Hogarth's young lady would probably
have cared little for this form of exercise,
even had the London policemen of 1748
been the chivalrous sufferers they were
in 1911. She is a buxom, demure dam-
sel ; and in her, as in the lad by her side,
there is a suggestion of reserve power.
They are citizens in the making, prepared
to accept soberly the restrictions and responsibilities of citizenship, and to follow
with relish the star of their own destinies.

And all things considered, what can be
better than to make a good job out of a
given piece of work? "That intricate web
of normal expectation," which Mr. Gilbert Murray tells us is the very essence
of human society, provides incentives for
reasonable men and women, and pro-

Counter-Currents

vides also compensations for courage.
What Mr. Murray calls a "failure of
nerve" in Greek philosophy and Greek
religion is the relaxing of effort, the letting down of obligation. With the ascet-
icism imposed, or at least induced, by
Christianity, "the sacrifice of one part of
human nature to another, that it may live
in what survives the more completely,"
he has but scant and narrow sympathy;
but he explains with characteristic clear-
ness that the ideals of Greek citizenship
withered and died, because of a weakening of faith in normal human resistance.
"All the last manifestations of Hellenistic
religion betray a lack of nerve."

It is with the best intentions in the
world that we Americans are now engaged in letting down the walls of human resistance, in lessening personal
obligation; and already the failure of
nerve is apparent on every side. We begin our kindly ministrations with the
little kindergarten scholar, to whom work

Our Loss of Nerve

is presented as play, and who is expected to absorb the elements of education without conscious effort, and certainly without compulsion. We encourage him to feel that the business of his teacher is to keep him interested in his task, and that he is justified in stopping short as soon as any mental process becomes irksome or difficult. Indeed, I do not know why I permit myself the use of the word "task," since by common consent it is banished from the vocabulary of school. Professor Gilman said it was a word which should never be spoken by teacher, never heard by pupil, and no doubt a kind-hearted public cordially agreed with him.

The firm old belief that the task is a valuable asset in education, that the making of a good job out of a given piece of work is about the highest thing on earth, has lost its hold upon the world. The firm old disbelief in a royal road to learning has vanished long ago. All knowledge, we are told, can be made so

Counter-Currents

attractive that school-children will absorb it with delight. If they are not absorbing it, the teacher is to blame. Professor Wiener tells us that when his precocious little son failed to acquire the multiplication tables, he took him away from school, and let him study advanced mathematics. Whereupon the child discovered the tables for himself. Mrs. John Macy, well known to the community as the friend and instructor of Miss Helen Keller, has informed a listening world that she does not see why a child should study *anything* in which he is not interested. "It is a waste of energy."

Naturally, it is hard to convince parents — who have the illusions common to their estate — that while exceptional methods may answer for exceptional cases (little William Pitt, for instance, was trained from early boyhood to be a prime minister), common methods have their value for the rank and file. It is harder still to make them understand

Our Loss of Nerve

that enjoyment cannot with safety be accepted as a determining factor in education, and that the mental and moral discipline which comes of hard and perhaps unwilling study is worth a mine of pleasantly acquired information. It is not, after all, a smattering of chemistry, or an acquaintance with the habits of bees, which will carry our children through life ; but a capacity for doing what they do not want to do, if it be a thing which needs to be done. They will have to do many things they do not want to do later on, if their lives are going to be worth the living, and the sooner they learn to stand to their guns, the better for them, and for all those whose welfare will lie in their hands.

The assumption that children should never be coerced into self-control, and never confronted with difficulties, makes for failure of nerve. The assumption that young people should never be burdened with responsibilities, and never, under any stress of circumstances, be deprived of the pleasures which are no longer a privilege, but their sacred and inalienable right, makes for failure of nerve. The assumption that married women are justified in abandoning their domestic duties, because they cannot stand the strain of home-life and housekeeping, makes for failure of nerve. The assumption that invalids must yield to invalidism, must isolate themselves from common currents of life, and from strong and stern incentives to recovery, makes for failure of nerve. The assumption that religion should content itself with persuasiveness, and that morality should be sparing in its demands, makes for failure of nerve. The assumption that a denial of civic rights constitutes a release from moral obligations makes for such a shattering failure of nerve that it brings insanity in its wake. And the assumption that poverty justifies prostitution, or exonerates the prostitute, lets down the last

Our Loss of Nerve

walls of human resistance. It is easier to find a royal road to learning than a royal road to self-mastery and self-respect.

A student of Mr. Whistler's once said to him that she did not want to paint in the low tones he recommended; she wanted to keep her colours clear and bright. "Then," replied Mr. Whistler, "you must keep them in your tubes. It is the only way." If we want bright colours and easy methods, we must stay in our tubes, and avoid the inevitable complications of life by careful and consistent uselessness. We may nurse our nerves in comfortable seclusion at home, or we may brace them with travel and change of scene. It does not matter; we are tube-dwellers under any skies. We may be so dependent upon amusements that we never call them anything but duties; or we may be as devout as La Fontaine's rat, which piously retired from the society of other rats into the heart of a Dutch cheese. We may be so rich that the world forgives us, or so poor that the world exonerates us. In each and every case we destroy life at the roots by a denial of its obligations, a fear of its difficulties, an indifference to its common rewards.

The seriousness of our age expresses itself in eloquent demands for gayety. The gospel of cheerfulness, I had almost said the gospel of amusement, is preached by people who lack experience to people who lack vitality. There is a vague impression that the world would be a good world if it were only happy, that it would be happy if it were amused, and that it would be amused if plenty of artificial recreation — that recreation for which we are now told every community stands responsible — were provided for its entertainment.

A few years ago an English clergyman made an eloquent appeal to the public, affirming that London's crying need was a score of "Pleasure-Palaces,"

Our Loss of Nerve

supported by taxpayers, and free as the Roman games. Gladiators being, indeed, out of date, lions costly, and martyrs very scarce, some milder and simpler form of diversion was to be substituted for the vigorous sports of Rome. Comic songs and acrobats were, in the reverend gentleman's opinion, the appointed agents for the regeneration of the London poor. It is worthy of note that the drama did not occur to him as a bigger and broader pastime. It is worthy of note that the drama is fast losing ground with the proletariat, once its staunch upholders. A very hard-thinking English writer, Mr. J. G. Leigh, sees in the substitution of cheap vaudeville for cheap melodrama an indication of what he calls loss of stamina, and of what Mr. Murray calls loss of nerve. "When the sturdy melodrama, with its foiled villainy and triumphant virtue, ceases to allure, and people want in its place the vulgar vapidities of the vaudeville, we may be sure there

Counter-Currents

is a spirit of sluggish impotence in the air."

To-day the moving pictures present the most triumphant form of cheap entertainment. They are good of their kind, and there is a visible effort to make them better; but the "special features" by which they are accompanied in the ten- and fifteen-cent shows, — the shrill songs, the dull jokes, the clumsy clog-dances, — are all of an incredible badness. Compared with them, the worst of plays seems good, and the ill-paid actors who storm and sob through "Alone in a Great City," or "No Wedding Bells for Her," assume heroic proportions, as ministering to the emotions of the heart.

The question of amusement is one with which all classes are deeply concerned. *Le Monde où l'on s'amuse* is no longer the narrow world of fashion. It has extended its border lines to embrace humanity. It is no longer an exclusively adult world. The pleasures of youth have

Our Loss of Nerve

become something too important for interference, too sacred for denial. Whatever may be happening to parents, whatever their cares and anxieties, the sons
and daughters must lose none of the gay-
eties now held essential to their happiness. They are trained to a selfishness
which is foreign to their natures, and
which does them grievous wrong. A few
years ago I asked an acquaintance about
her mother, with whom she lived, and
who was, I knew, incurably ill. "She is
no better," said the lady disconsolately,
"and I must say it is very hard on my
children. They cannot have any of their
young friends in the house. They cannot
entertain. They have been cut off from
all social pleasures this winter."

I said it was a matter of regret, and
I forbore to add that the poor invalid
would probably have been glad to die
a little sooner, had she been given the
chance. It was not the mere selfishness
of old age which kept her so long about

it. Yet neither was my acquaintance the callous creature that she seemed. Left to herself, she would not have begrudged her mother the time to die; but she had been deeply imbued with the conviction that young people in general, and her own children in particular, should never be saddened, or depressed, or asked to assume responsibilities, or be called upon for self-denial. She was preparing them carefully for that failure of nerve which would make them impotent in the stress of life.

The desire of the modern philanthropist to provide amusement for the working-classes is based upon the determination of the working classes to be amused. He is as keen that the poor shall have their fill of dancing, as Dickens, in his less enlightened age, was keen that the poor should have their fill of beer. He knows that it is natural for young men and women to crave diversion, and that it is right for them to have it. What

Our Loss of Nerve

he does not clearly understand, what Dickens did not clearly understand, is that to crave either amusement or drink so weakly that we cannot conquer our craving, is to be worthless in a work-a-day world.

And worse than worthless in a world which is called upon for heroism and high resolve. A cruel lesson taught by the war is the degeneracy of the British workman, who, in the hour of his country's need, has clung basely to his ease and his sottishness. What does it avail that English gentlemen fling away their lives with unshrinking courage, when the common people, from whose sturdy spirit England was wont to draw her strength, have shrivelled into a craven apathy. The contempt of the British soldier for the British artisan is not the contempt of the fighting man for the man of peace. It is the loathing of the man who has accepted his trust for the man who can do and bear nothing ; who cries out

Counter-Currents

if his drink is touched, who cries out if his work is heavy, who cries out if his hours are lengthened, who has parted with his manhood, and does not want it back. Whatever England has needed for the regeneration of her sons, it was certainly not " pleasure-palaces " and cheap amusements. The "sluggish impotence" which Mr. Leigh observed four years ago, did not call, and does not call, for relaxation. The only cure will be so stern that no one cares to prophesy its coming.

And Americans! Well, thousands of people bearing that name assembled in New York on the 13th of November, 1915, under the auspices of the Woman's Peace Party, and amused themselves by denouncing the Administration, howling down all mention of national defence, and jeering every time the word patriotism (which we used to think a noble word) was spoken in their hearing. Men endeared themselves to the audience by declaring that they would not risk their

Our Loss of Nerve

all too precious lives to fight for any cause, and women intelligently asked why a foreign rule would not be just as good as a home one. They did not seem aware that Brussels was having a less enviable time than Boston or Milwaukee. Profound foolishness swayed the audience, abysmal ignorance soothed it. There was an abundant showing of childish irrationality; there was the apathy which befits old age; but of intelligence or of virility there was nothing.

This loss of nerve, this "weakening of faith in normal human resistance," means the disintegration of citizenship. It is the sudden call to manhood which shows us where manhood is not to be found. We Americans, begirt by sentiment, mindful of our ease, and spared for more than half-a-century from ennobling self-sacrifice, have been seeking smooth and facile methods of reform. The world, grown old in ill-doing, responds nimbly to our offers of amusement, but balks at the austere virtues which no cajolery can disguise. The more it is amused, the more it assumes amusement to be its due; and this assumption receives the support and encouragement of those whose experience must have taught them its perils.

Miss Jane Addams, in her careful study of the Chicago streets, speaks of the "pleasure-loving girl who demands that each evening shall bring her some measure of recreation." Miss Addams admits that such a girl is beset by nightly dangers, but does not appear to think her attitude an unnatural or an unreasonable one. A very able and intelligent woman who has worked hard for the establishment of decently conducted dance-halls in New York, — dance-halls sorely needed to supplant the vicious places of entertainment where drink and degradation walk hand in hand, — was asked at a public meeting whether the girls for whose welfare she was pleading never

Our Loss of Nerve

stayed at home. "Never," was the firm
reply, "and will you pardon me for saying, Neither do you." The retort provoked laughter, because the young married woman who had put the question
probably never did spend a night at
home, unless she were entertaining. She
represented a social summit, — a combi-
nation of health, wealth, beauty, charm
and high spirits. But there were scores
of girls and women in the audience
who spent many nights at home. There
are hundreds of girls and women in
what are called fashionable circles who
spend many nights at home. There are
thousands of girls and women in more
modest circumstances who spend many
nights at home. If this were not the case,
our cities would soon present a spectacle of demoralization. They would be
chaotic on the surface, and rotten at the
core.

It is claimed that the nervous exhaustion produced by hours of sustained and

Counter-Currents

monotonous labour sends the factory girl into the streets at night. She is too unstrung for rest. That this is in a measure true, no experienced worker will deny, because every experienced worker is familiar with the sensation. Every woman who has toiled for hours, whether with a sewing machine or a typewriter, whether with a needle or a pen, whether in an office or at home, has felt the nervous fatigue which does not crave rest but distraction, which makes her want to " go." Every woman worth her salt has overcome this weakness, has mastered this desire. It is probable that many men suffer and struggle in the same fashion. Dr. Johnson certainly did. With inspired directness, he speaks of people who are "afraid to go home and think." He knew that fear. Many a night it drove him through the London streets till daybreak. He conquered it, conquered the sick nerves so at variance with his sound mind and sound princi-

Our Loss of Nerve

ples, and his example is a beacon light to strugglers in the gloom.

Naturally, the working girl knows nothing about Dr. Johnson. Unhappily, she knows little of any beacon light or guide. But, if she be a reasonable human being, she *does* know that to expect every evening to "bring her some measure of recreation" is an utterly unreasonable demand, and that it can be gratified only at the risk of her physical and moral undoing. She has been taught to read in our public schools; she is provided with countless novels and storybooks by our public libraries; the lightest of light literature is at her command. Is this not enough to tide her over a night or two in the week? If her clothes never need mending or renovating, she is unlike any other woman the world has got to show. If there is never any washing, ironing, or housework for her to do, her position is at once unusual and regrettable. If she will not sometimes read,

Counter-Currents

or work, or, because she is tired, go early to bed ; if her craving for amusement has reached that acute stage when only the streets, or the moving pictures, or the dance-hall will satisfy it, she has so completely lost nerve that she has no moral stamina left. She may be virtuous, but she is an incapable weakling, and the working man who marries her ruins his life. Such girls swell the army of deserted wives which is the despair of all organized charities.

The sincere effort to regenerate the world by amusing it is to be respected ; but it is not the final word of reform. The sincere effort to regenerate the world by a legal regulation of wages is a new version of an old story, — the shifting of personal obligation, the search for somebody's door at which to lay the burden of blame. It is also a denial of human experience, inherited and acquired, and a rejection of the only doctrine which stands for self-respect: " Temptations do

Our Loss of Nerve

not make the man, but they show him for what he is." Qualities nourished by this stern and sane doctrine die with the withering of faith.

So much well-meant, but not harmless nonsense — nonsense is never harmless — has been preached concerning women and their wages, that we are in the predicament of Sydney Smith when Macaulay flooded him with talk. We positively "stand in the slops." A professor of economics in an American college offers out of the fulness of his heart the following specific and original remedy for existing ills: "My idea is that one of the best ways to get an increased remuneration for women is to make them worth it."

"My idea!" This is what it means to have the scientific mind at work. A unique proposition (what have we been thinking about with our free schools for the past hundred years?), unclogged by detail, unhampered by ways and means. And if we do not see salvation in truisms,

Counter-Currents

if we are daunted by the gulf between people who are theorizing and people who are merely living, we can take refuge with the reformers who demand "increased remuneration for women" whether they are worth it or not; who would make the need of the worker, and not the quality of the work, the determining factor in wages. We may "protect women from themselves," by prohibiting them from accepting less than their legal hire.

The only real peril of a minimum wage law is that it has a tendency to relegate the incompetent to beggary. It cannot, as some economists claim, discourage efficiency. Nothing can discourage efficiency, which scorns help and defies hindrance. But, by the same ruling, nothing can command more than it is worth in the markets of the world. We do wrong when we release the worker from any incentive to good work. We do wrong when we release her from a sense of per-

Our Loss of Nerve

sonal responsibility. We do wrong when we give her a plausible excuse for following the line of least resistance, when we blight her courage by permitting her to think that her moral welfare lies in any hands but her own. The choice between poverty and dishonesty, the choice between poverty and prostitution is not an "open question." It is closed, if human reason and human experience can speak authoritatively upon any subject in the world.

The injury done by loose thinking and loose talking is irremediable. When the State Senate Vice Investigating Committee of Illinois permitted and encouraged an expression of what it was pleased to call the "shop-girl's philosophy," it sowed the seeds of mischief deep enough to insure a heavy crop of evil. I quote a single episode, as it was reported in the newspapers of March 8th, 1913, — a report which, if inaccurate in detail, must be correct in substance. A young wo-

Counter-Currents

man who had been in the employ of Sears, Roebuck & Co. was on the stand. She was questioned by Lieutenant-Governor O'Hara.

"'If a girl were getting $8 a week, and had to support a widowed mother, would you blame that girl if she committed a crime?'

"The witness looked up frankly, and replied, 'No, I would n't.'

"'Would you blame her if she killed herself?'

"'No, I would n't,' came the emphatic reply.

"'And would you blame her, if she committed a greater crime?'

"The young Lieutenant-Governor's meaning was in his embarrassed tones and in his heightened colour. The girl was the more composed of the two. She paused a moment, and then repeated distinctly, 'No, I would n't.'

"The room had been painfully quiet, but at this there was a round of applause,

58

Our Loss of Nerve

led by the women spectators. It was the first general spontaneous outburst of the session. 'Emily' was then dismissed."

Dismissed with the "round of applause" ringing in her ears, and in her mind the comfortable assurance that her theory of life was a sound one. Also that a warm-hearted public was prepared to exonerate her, should she find a virtuous life too onerous for endurance. Is it likely that this girl, and hundreds of other Emilys, thus encouraged to let down the walls of resistance, can be saved from the hopeless failure of nerve which will relegate them to the ranks of the defeated? Is it likely that the emotional hysteria of the applauding audience, and of hundreds of similar audiences, can be reduced to reason by such sober statistics as those furnished by the Bureau of Social Hygiene in New York, or by the New York State Reformatory for Women at Bedford Hills? Less than three per cent of seven hundred girls exam-

Counter-Currents

ined at the Bedford Hills reformatory pleaded poverty as a reason for their fall; and, of this three per cent, more than half had been temporarily out of work. On the other hand, twenty per cent were feeble-minded, were mentally incapacitated for self-control, and as much at the mercy of their instincts as so many animals. These are the blameless unfortunates whom vice commissioners seem somewhat disposed to ignore. These are the women who should be protected from themselves, and from whose progeny the public should be protected.

It is evident that triumphant virtue must have strong foundations. Income and recreation are but slender props. Becky Sharp was of the opinion that, given five thousand pounds a year, she could be as respectable as her neighbours; but, in our hearts, we have always doubted Becky. "Where virtue is well rooted," said the watchful Saint

Our Loss of Nerve

Theresa, "provocations matter little." All results are in proportion to the greatness of the spirit which has nourished them. When Cromwell made the discomforting discovery that "tapsters and town apprentices" could not stand in battle against the Cavaliers, he said to his cousin, John Hampden, that he must have men of religion to fight with men of honour. He summoned these men of religion, fired them with enthusiasm, hardened them into consistency, and within fourteen years the nations which had mocked learned to fear, and the name of England was "made terrible" to the world.

For big issues we must have strong incentives and compelling measures. "Where the religious emotions surge up," says Mr. Gilbert Murray, "the moral emotions are not far away." Perhaps the mighty forces which have winnowed the world for centuries may still prove efficacious. Perhaps the illuminating principles of religion, the ennobling spirit of patriotism, the uncompromising standards of morality, may do more to stiffen our powers of resistance than lectures on "Life as a Fine Art," or papers on "The Significance of Play," and "Amusement as a Factor in Man's Spiritual Uplift." Perhaps the stable government which ensures to the Industrious Apprentice the reward of his own diligence is more bracing to citizenship than the zealous humanity which protects the Idle Apprentice from the consequences of his own ill-doing.

Christianity and War

THERE are two disheartening features in the attitude of Americans toward the ruthless war which has been waged in Europe for the past two years. One is the materialism of pacifists who ignore, and have steadily ignored, the crucial question of right and wrong, justice and injustice. The other is the materialism of pious Christians who lament the failure of Christianity to reconcile the irreconcilable, to preserve the long-threatened security of nations.

When, at the request of President Wilson, the first Sunday of October, 1914, was set aside as a day of prayer for peace, — a day of many sermons and of many speeches, — prayers and sermons and speeches all alluded to the war as though it were the cholera or the plague, something simple of issue, the abatement of which would mean people getting better, the cure of which would mean people getting well. The possibility of a peace shameful to justice and disastrous to civilization was carefully ignored. The truth that death is better than a surrender of all that makes life morally worth the living, was never spoken. This may be what neutrality implies. We addressed the Almighty in guarded language lest He should misunderstand our position. We listened respectfully when Secretary Bryan told us that our first duty was to use what influence we might have to hasten the return of peace, without asking him to be more explicit, to say what on earth he would have had us do, and how — without moving hand or foot — he would have had us do it.

Since then, men of little faith have kept dinning in our ears that religion is eclipsed, that Gospel law lacks the sub-

Christianity and War

stance of a dream, that Christian principles are bankrupt in the hour of need, that the only God now worshipped in Europe is the tribal God who fights for his own people, and that the structure of love and duty, reared by centuries of Christianity, has toppled into ruin. To quote Professor Cramb's classic phrase, "Corsica has conquered Galilee." Some of these sad-minded prophets had fathers and grandfathers who fought in the Civil War, and they seem in no wise troubled by this distressful fact. Some of them had great-great-grandfathers who fought in the Revolutionary War, and *they* join high-sounding societies out of illogical pride. Yet the colonists who defended their freedom and their new-born national life were not more justified in shedding blood, than were the French and Belgians and Serbians who heroically defended their invaded countries and their shattered homes.

When Mr. Carnegie thanked God

Counter-Currents

(through the medium of the newspapers) that he lived in a brotherhood of nations, —"forty-eight nations in one Union," — he forgot that these forty-eight nations, or at least thirty-eight of them, were not always a brotherhood. Nor was the family tie preserved by moral suasion. What we of the North did was to beat our brothers over the head until they consented to be brotherly. And some three hundred thousand of them died of grievous wounds and fevers rather than love us as they should.

This was termed preserving the Union. The abiding gain is visible to all men, and it is not our habit to question the methods employed for its preservation. No one called or calls the " Battle Hymn of the Republic" a cry to a tribal God, although it very plainly tells the Lord that his place is with the Federal, and not with the Confederate lines. And when the unhappy Belgians crowded the Cathedral of St. Gudule, asking Heav-

Christianity and War

en's help for defenceless Brussels, imploring the intercession of our Lady of Deliverance (pitiful words that wring the heart!), was this a cry to a tribal God, or the natural appeal of humanity to a power higher and more merciful than man? Americans returning from war-stricken Europe in the autumn of 1914 spoke unctuously of their country as "God's own land," by which they meant a land where their luggage was unmolested. But it is possible that nations fighting with their backs to the wall for all they hold sacred and dear are as justified in the sight of God as a nation smugly content with its own safety, living its round of pleasures, giving freely of its superfluity, and growing rich with the vast increase of its industries and trade.

What influence has been at work since the close of the Franco-Prussian War, shutting our eyes to the certainty of that war's final issue, and debauching our minds with sentiment which had no truth to rest on? We knew that the taxes of Europe were spent on armaments, and we talked about International Arbitration. We knew that science was devotedly creating ruthless instruments of destruction, and we turned our pleased attention to the beautiful ceremonies with which the Peace Palace at The Hague was dedicated. We knew, or we might have known, that the strategic railway built by Germany to carry troops to the Belgian frontier was begun in 1904, and that the memorandum of General Schlieffen was sanctioned by the Emperor (there was no pretence of secrecy) in 1909. Yet we thought—in common with the rest of the world—that a "scrap of paper" and a plighted word would constitute protection. We knew that Germany's answer to England's proposals for a mutual reduction of navies was an increase of estimates, and a double number of dreadnoughts.

Christianity and War

Did we suppose these dreadnoughts were
playthings for the Imperial nurseries?

"A pretty toy," quoth she, "the Thunderer's
  bolt!
My urchins play with it."

When in 1911 President Taft's "message" was hailed as a prophecy of
peace, Germany's reply was spoken by
Bethmann-Hollweg: "The vital strength
of a nation is the only measure of a nation's armaments."

And now the good people who for
years have been saying that war is archaic, are reproaching Christianity for
not making it impossible. Did not the
"American Association for International
Conciliation" issue comforting pamphlets, entitled "The Irrationality of
War," and "War Practically Prevent-
able"? That ought to have settled the
matter forever. Did we not appoint a
"Peace Day" for our schools, and a
"Peace Sunday" for churches and Sunday schools? Did not Mr. Carnegie pay

ten millions down for international peace,
—and get a very poor article for his
money? There were some beautiful papers read to the Peace Congress at The
Hague, just twelve months before Europe was in flames; and there is the report of a commission of inquiry which
the "World Peace Foundation," formerly the "International School of
Peace," informed us three years ago
was "a great advance toward assured
peaceful relations between nations."

With this sea of sentiment billowing
about us, and with Nobel prizes drop-
ping like gentle rain from Heaven upon
thirsty peace-lovers, how should we read
the signs of war, written in the language
of artillery? It is true that President
Nicholas Murray Butler, speaking in
behalf of the Carnegie Peace Foundation, observed musingly in November,
1913, that there was no visible interest
displayed by any foreign government,
or by any responsible foreign statesman,

Christianity and War

in the preparations for the Third Hague Conference, scheduled for 1915 ; but this was not a matter for concern. It was more interesting to read about the photographs of " educated and humane men and women," which the " World Conference for Promoting Concord between all Divisions of Mankind " (a title that leaves nothing, save grammar, to be desired) proposed collecting in a vast and honoured album for the edification of the peaceful earth.

And all this time England — England, with her life at stake — shared our serene composure. Lord Salisbury, indeed, and Lord Roberts cherished no illusions concerning Germany's growing power and ultimate intentions. But then Lord Roberts was a soldier ; and Lord Salisbury, though outwitted in the matter of Heligoland, had that quality of mistrust which is always so painful in a statesman. The English press preferred, on the whole, to reflect the opinions of Lord

Counter-Currents

Haldane. They were amiable and soothing. Lord Haldane knew the Kaiser, and
deemed him a friendly man. Had he not
cried harder than anybody else at Queen
Victoria's funeral? Lord Haldane had
translated Schopenhauer, and could afford to ignore Treitschke. None of the
German professors with whom he was
on familiar terms were of the Treitschke
mind. They were all friendly men. It is
true that Germany, far from talking plati-
tudes about peace, has for years past defined with amazing lucidity and candour
her doctrine that might is right. She is
strong, brave, covetous, she has what is
called in urbane language "the instinct
for empire," and she follows implicitly

"The good old rule, . . . the simple plan,
That they should take who have the power,
And they should keep who can."

It was forlornly amusing to see, three
months after the declaration of war, our
book-shops filled with cheap copies of
General von Bernhardi's bellicose vol-

Christianity and War

ume; to open our newspapers, and find column after column of quotation from it; to pick up our magazines, and discover that all the critics were busy discussing it. That book was published in 1911, and the world (outside of Germany which took its text to heart) remained "more than usual calm." Its forcible and closely knit argument is defined and condensed in one pregnant sentence: "The notion that a weak nation has the same right to live as a powerful nation is a presumptuous encroachment on the natural law of development."

This is something different from the suavities of peace-day orators. It is also vastly different from the sentiments so gently expressed by General von Bernhardi in his more recent volume, dictated by German diplomacy, and designed as a tract for the United States and other neutral nations. Soothing syrup is not sweeter than this second book; but its laboured explanations, its

Counter-Currents

amiable denials, even the pretty compliment paid us by a quotation from " A Psalm of Life " (why ignore " Mary had a little lamb "?), have failed to obliterate the sharp, clear outlines of his pitiless policy. Being now on the safe side of prophecy, we wag our heads over the amazing exactitude with which Bernhardi forecast Germany's impending war. But there was at least one English student and observer, Professor J. A. Cramb of Queen's College, London, who gave plain and unheeded warning of the fast-deepening peril, and of the life-or-death struggle which England would be compelled to face. Step by step he traced the expansion of German nationalism, which since 1870 has never swerved from its stern military ideals. A reading people, the Germans. Yes, and in a single year they published seven hundred books dealing with war as a science, — not one of them written for a prize! If the weakness of Germany lies in her assumption that there is no such thing as honour or integrity in international relations, her strength lies in her reliance on her own carefully measured efficiency. Her contempt for other nations has kept pace with the distrust she inspires.

The graceful remark of a Prussian official to Matthew Arnold, "It is not so much that we dislike England, as that we think little of her," was the expression of a genuine Teutonic sentiment. So, too, was General von Bernhardi's characteristic sneer at the "childlike" confidence reposed by Mr. Elihu Root and his friends in the Hague High Court of International Justice, with public opinion at its back. Of what worth, he asked, is law that cannot be converted by force into government? What is the weight of opinion, unsupported by the glint of arms? Professor Cramb, seeing in Bernhardi, and in his great master, Treitschke, the inspiration of their country's high ambition, told England in the plainest words he could command that just as the old German Imperialism began with the destruction of Rome, so would the new German Imperialism begin with the destruction of England; and that if Englishmen dreamed of security from attack, they were destined to a terrible and bloody awakening. Happily for himself, — since he was a man too old and ill to fight, — he died nine months before the fulfilment of his prophecy.

Now that the inevitable has come to pass, now that the armaments have been put to the use for which they were always intended, and the tale of battle is too terrible to be told, press and pulpit are calling Christianity to account for its failure to preserve peace. Ethical societies are reminding us, with something which sounds like elation, that they have long pointed out "the relaxed hold of doctrine on the minds of the educated classes." How they love that phrase, "educated classes," and what, one won-

Christianity and War

ders, do they mean by it? A Jewish rabbi, speaking in Carnegie hall, laments, or rejoices — it is hard to tell which — that Christian Churches are not taken, and do not take themselves, seriously. Able editors comment in military language upon the inability of religious forces to "mobilize" rapidly and effectively in the interests of peace, and turn out neat phrases like "anti-Christian Christendom," which are very effective in editorials. Popular preachers, too broad-minded to submit to clerical authority, deliver "syndicated sermons," denouncing the "creeds of the Dark Ages," which still, in these electricity-lighted days, pander to war. Worse than all, troubled men, seeing the world suddenly bereft of justice and of mercy, lose courage, and whisper in the silence of their own sad hearts, "There is no God."

Meanwhile, the assaulted churches take, as is natural, somewhat conflicting views of the situation. Roman Catho-

Counter-Currents

lics have been disposed to think that the persecutions of the Church in France are bearing bitter fruit; and at least one American Cardinal has spoken of the war as God's punishment for this offence. But if the Almighty appointed Belgium to be the whipping boy for the sins of France, we shall have to revise our notions of divine justice and beneficence. Belgium is the most Catholic country in Europe. Hundreds of the priests and nuns expelled from France found shelter within its frontiers. But if it were as stoutly Lutheran or Calvinistic, it would be none the less innocent of France's misdemeanours. Moreover, it is worthy of note that French priests, far from moralizing over the situation, have rallied to their country's call. The bugbear, " clerical peril," has dropped out of sight. In its place are confidence on the one side, and unstinted devotion on the other. Exiled monks have returned to fight in the French army. Students of

Christianity and War

theological seminaries have been no less keen than other students to take up arms for France. Abbés have served as sergeants and ensigns, dying as cheerfully as other men in the monotonous carnage on the Aisne. Wounded priests have shrived their wounded comrades on the battlefield. Everywhere the clergy are playing manly and patriotic parts, forgetting what wrong was done them, remembering what name they bear.

England, with more precision, outlined her views in the manifesto issued September 29, 1914, and designed as a reply to those German theologians who had asked English "Evangelical Christians" to hold back their hands from bloodshed. The manifesto was signed by Bishops and Archbishops of the Church of England, and by leading Nonconformists, all of whom found themselves for once in heartfelt amity. It is a plain-spoken document, declaring that truth and honour (it might have added safety)

are better things than peace; and that
Christian England endorses without res-
ervation the rightness of the war. One
of the signers, the Bishop of London, is
chaplain to the London Rifle Brigade.
No doubt about *his* sentiments. The
words of another, the Archbishop of
York, are simple, sincere, and pleasantly
free from patronage of the Almighty. "I
dare to say that we can carry this cause
without shame or misgiving into the pres-
ence of Him who is the Judge of the
whole earth, and ask Him to bless it."

As for Germany, it may be, as some
enthusiasts assert, that her "creative
power in religion," keeping pace with
her "genius for empire," will turn her
out a brand-new faith, the "world-faith"
foreseen by Treitschke, a religion of
valour and of unceasing effort. Or it
may be that the God of her fathers will
content her, seeing that she leaves Him
so little to do. Like Cromwell, who was
a religious man (his thanksgiving for the

Christianity and War

massacre at Drogheda was as heartfelt as any offered by the Kaiser, or by the Kaiser's grandfather), Germany keeps her powder dry.

Christianity and war have walked together down the centuries. How could it be otherwise? We have to reckon with humanity, and humanity is not made over every hundred years. Science has multiplied instruments of destruction, but the heart of the soldier is the same. It is an anachronism, this human heart, just as war is an anachronism, but it still beats. Nothing sacred and dear could have survived upon the earth had men not fought for their women, their homes, their individual honour, and their national life. And while men stay men, they must give up their lives when the hour strikes. How shall they believe that, dying on the frontiers of their invaded countries, or at the gates of their besieged towns, they sin against the law of Christ?

Counter-Currents

Heroism is good for the soul, and it bears as much practical fruit as law-making. It goes further in moulding and developing the stuff of which a great nation is made. "There is a flower of honour, there is a flower of chivalry, there is a flower of religion." So Sainte-Beuve equips the spirit of man; and the soldier, no less than the civilian, cherishes this threefold bloom. Because he "lives dangerously," he feels the need of God. Because his life is forfeit, there is about him the dignity of sacrifice. Anna Robeson Burr, in her volume on "The Autobiography," quotes an illustrative passage from the Commentaries of that magnificent fighter and lucid writer, Blaise de Monluc, maréchal de France: "Que je me trouve, en voyant les ennemis, en telle peur que je sentois le cœur et les membres s'affoiblir et trembler. Puis, ayant dit mes petites prières latines, je sentois tout–à–coup venir un chaleur au cœur et aux membres."

Christianity and War

"Petites prières latines!" A monkish patter. And this was a man belonging to the "educated classes," and a citizen of the world. Sully, in his memoirs, tells us that, at the siege of Montmélian, a cannon-shot struck the ground close to the spot where he and the king were standing, showering upon them earth and little flint stones; whereupon Henry swiftly and unconsciously made the sign of the cross. "Now I know," said the delighted Sully, — himself an unswerving Protestant, — "now I know that you are a good Catholic."

We must always reckon with humanity, unless, indeed, we are orators, living in a world of words, and marshalling unconquerable theories against unconquered facts. The French priest at Soissons who distributed to the Turcos little medals of the Blessed Virgin may not have been an advanced thinker, but he displayed a pleasant acquaintance with mankind. There was no time to explain

to these unbelievers the peculiar efficacy
of the medals; for that he trusted to Our
Lady; but their presentation was a link
between the Catholic soldier and the
Moslem, who were fighting side by side
for France. Perhaps this priest remembered that close at hand, in the hamlet
of Saint-Médard, lie the relics of Saint
Sebastian, Christian gentleman and martyr, who was an officer in the imperial
bodyguard of Diocletian, rendering to
Cæsar the service that was Cæsar's, until
the hour came for him to render to God
the life that was always God's.

The wave of religious emotion which
sweeps over a nation warring for its life
is not the mere expression of that nation's sharpened needs; it is not only a
cry for help where help is sorely needed.
It is part of man's responsiveness to the
call of duty, his sense of self-sacrifice in
giving his body to death in order that
his country may live. "Religion," says
Mr. Stephen Graham, "is never shaken

Christianity and War

down by war. The intellectual dominance is shaken and falls; the spiritual powers are allowed to take possession of men's beings." That a truth so simple and so often illustrated should fail to be understood, proves the torpor of materialism. A sad-minded American writer, commenting on the destruction of the Cathedral of Rheims, made the amazing discovery that the sorrow and indignation evoked by this national crime showed an utter collapse of Christianity. Every one, he said, bewailed the loss to the world. No one bewailed the loss to religion. Therefore faith lay dead.

That religion can lose nothing by the destruction of her monuments is the solace of Christian souls. Her churches lie in crumbling ruins. Ypres, Pervyse, Soissons, Revigny, Souain, Maurupt, Étavigny. Everywhere stand the shattered walls of what was once a church, with here and there an altar burned or hacked, and a mutilated crucifix. But the faith that built these churches is as unassailable as the souls of the men who died for them. There are things beyond the reach of "high explosives," and it is not for them we grieve.

It is a common saying that the New Testament affords no vindication of war, which is natural enough, not being penned as a manual for nations. But Catholic theology, having been called on very early to pronounce judgment upon this recurrent incident of life, has defined with absolute exactitude what, in the eyes of the Church, justifies, and what necessitates war. From a mass of minute detail, — laws laid down by Saint Thomas Aquinas and other doctors of the Church, — I venture to quote two salient points, the first dealing with the nature of a right, the second with the nature of a title.

"Every perfect right, that is, every right involving in others an obligation in justice of deference thereto, if it is to

Christianity and War

be an efficacious, and not an illusory power, carries with it as a last appeal the subsidiary right of coercion. A perfect right, then, implies the right of physical force to defend itself against infringement, to recover the subject-matter of right unjustly withheld, or to exact its equivalent, and to inflict damage in the exercise of this coercion, wherever coercion cannot be exercised without such damage."

"The primary title of a state to go to war is, first, the fact that the state's rights are menaced by foreign aggression not otherwise to be prevented than by war; second, the fact of actual violation of right not otherwise reparable; third, the need of punishing the threatening or invading power, for the security of the future. From the nature of the proved right, those three facts are necessarily just titles, and the state whose rights are in jeopardy is itself the judge thereof."

I am aware that theology is not popular, save with theologians; but after reading Treitschke and Bernhardi on the one hand, and the addresses delivered at "peace demonstrations" on the other, it is inexpressibly refreshing to follow straight thought instead of crooked thought, or words that hold no thought at all. I am also aware that Catholic wars have not always been waged along the lines laid down by Catholic theology; but this is beside the point. The Mosaic law was not the less binding upon the Jews because they were always breaking it. Nor are we prepared to say that they would have been as sound morally without a law so constantly infringed. It is well to know that, even in the spirit, there is such a thing as justice and admitted right.

To prate about the wickedness of war without drawing a clear line of demarcation between aggressive and defensive warfare, between violating a treaty and upholding it, is to lose our mental bal-

Christianity and War

ance, to substitute sentiment for truth.
The very wrongness of the one implies
logically the rightness of the other. And
whatever is morally right is in accord
with Christianity. To speak loosely of
war as unchristian is to ignore not only
the Christian right, but the Christian
duty, which rests with every nation and
with every man to protect that of which
nation and man are lawful protectors.
Even aggressive warfare is not necessarily a denial of the Christianity it affronts.
Crooked thinking comes naturally to
men, and the power of self-deception is
without bounds. God is not deceived;
but the instinctive desire of the creature
to hoodwink the Creator, to induce Him
— for a consideration — to compound a
felony, is revealed in every page of history, and under every aspect of civilization. The necessity which man has always felt of being on speaking terms
with his own conscience, built churches
and abbeys in the days of faith, and en-

dows educational institutions in this day of enlightenment; but it very imperfectly controlled, or controls, the actions of men or of nations. If our confidence in the future were not based upon ignorance of the past, we should better understand, and more courageously face, the harsh realities of life.

Two lessons taught by the war are easily learned. There is no safety in talk, and there is no assurance that the world's heritage of beauty, its triumphs of art and of architecture, will descend to our children and our grandchildren. We never reckoned on this loss of our common inheritance. We never thought that the gracious gifts made by the far past to the dim future could be so speedily destroyed, and that a single day would suffice to impoverish all coming generations. What can the pedantry, the "culture," of the twentieth century give to compensate us for the loss of Rheims Cathedral? The deficit is too heavy to

Christianity and War

be counted. Not France alone, but the civilized world, has been robbed beyond measure and beyond retrievement. Life is less good to all of us, and will be less good to those who come after us, because this great sacrilege has been committed. As for culture, — the careful destruction of the University of Louvain proves once and forever that scholarship is no more sacred than art or than religion, when the tide of invasion breaks upon a doomed and helpless land.

This affords food for thought. Italy, for example, is the treasure-house of the world. She is the guardian of the beauty she created, and to her shrine goes all mankind in pilgrimage. How long would her cathedrals, her palaces, her galleries, survive assault? What would be left of Venice after a week's bombardment? What of Florence, or of Rome? There is no such thing as safety in war. There is no such thing as safety in neutrality. Italy has more to lose than all the other nations of Europe, and is there one of us who would not be a partner in her loss?

And the United States? "God's own land"? Are we forever secure? True we have little to fear in the destruction of our public monuments, which are rather like the public monuments of Prussia, the ornate edifices and ramping statues of Hamburg and Berlin. It might be a pious duty to let them go. But we have homes which are as precious to us as were once the devastated homes of Belgium to happy men and women; and we confide their safety to treaties, to scraps of paper, like the one which made Belgium inviolate. If we are in search of life's ironies, let us note that a Roman Catholic Peace Conference was to have been convened in Liège, the very month that Germany struck her blow. A fortnight's delay, and delegates might have been making speeches on the concord of nations, while the streets of Aerschot

Christianity and War

ran blood, and Wespelaer was looted and burned.

Yet so deep-rooted is sentiment in our souls, so averse are we to facing facts, that to-day a " peace meeting " will pack a convention hall in any town of any state in the Union. We are as pleased to hear that "the brotherhood of man is the only basis for enduring peace among the nations " as if this shadowy brotherhood had taken form and substance. We listen with undiminished trustfulness to Mr. Bryan's oft-repeated plans for ending the war by remonstrating soberly with the warriors. We see hope in conferences, in speeches, in telegrams to Washington, in appeals " from the mothers of the nation." How many months have passed since Mr. La Follette evoked our enthusiastic response to these well-timed, well-balanced words? " The accumulated and increasing horrors of the European wars are creating a great tidal wave of public opinion that sweeps aside all specious reasoning, and admits of but one simple, common-sense, humane conclusion, — a demand for peace and disarmament among civilized nations."

To this we all cried Amen! But as there was nobody to bell the cat, the war went bloodily on. The question who was to "demand" peace, and of whom it was to be demanded, was one which Mr. La Follette could not, or at least did not, answer. "Public opinion" has a weighty sound. All our lives we have pinned our faith to this bodiless thing, and it has failed us in our need. Why, if it can work miracles in the future, should it have been so helpless in these two sad years? The Hague Conference of 1907 laid down definite rules of warfare, — rules to which the nations of Europe subscribed with cheerful unanimity. They forbade pillage, the levying of indemnities, the seizure of funds belonging to local authorities, collective penalties for individual acts, the conveying of

Christianity and War

troops or munitions across the territory
of a neutral power, and all terrorization
of a country by harshness to its civilian
population. The object of these rules,
every one of which has been broken in
Belgium, was to keep war within the
limits set by what Mr. Henry James
calls the "high decency" of Christian
civilization. Public opinion has been as
powerless to enforce the least of these
rules as it has been powerless to prevent
the sinking of unarmed merchant ships,
the drowning of men, women and children belonging to neutral nations. How
can we hope that a force so feeble to-
day will control the world to-morrow?

If the Allies emerge triumphantly from
the war, and England demands the reduction of armaments, then this good
result will have been gained by desperate fighting, not by noble sentiments.
We, whose sentiments have been of the
noblest, shall have had no real share in
the work. If Germany conquers, and

Counter-Currents

stands unassailable, a great military
world-power, fired with a sense of her
exalted destiny, rich with the spoils of
Europe, and holding in her mailed hands
the power to enforce her will, is it at all
likely that our excellent arguments will
prevail upon her to reverse her policy,
and enfeeble herself for our safety? A
successful aggressive warfare does not
pave the way to a lasting and honourable peace. This is one of the truths we
may learn, if we will, from history.

For years we have chosen to believe
that arbitration would ensure for the
world a maximum of comfort at a minimum of cost, and that the religion of
humanity would achieve what the religion of Christ has never achieved, —
the mythical brotherhood of man. From
this dream we have been rudely awakened; but, being awake, let us at least
recognize and respect that simple and
great quality which makes every man
the defender of his home, the guardian

Christianity and War

of his rights, the avenger of his shameful wrongs.

We, too, have fought bravely in our day. We, too, have known what it is to do all that man can do, and to bear all that man must bear; and it was not in the hour of our trial that we talked about bankrupt Christianity. When Serbia made her choice between death and the uttermost dishonour, she vindicated the sacred right of humanity. When Belgium with incredible courage defended her own good name and the safety of France, she stood erect before God and man, and laid down her life for her friend.

Women and War

THE only agreeable thing to be recorded in connection with Europe's sudden and disastrous war is the fact that people stopped talking about women, and began to talk about men. For the past decade, women have persistently occupied the front of the stage, and men have seemed a negligible factor; useful in their imperfect way, but hopelessly unproblematic. Then Austria delivered her ultimatum, Germany marched her armies across a peaceful earth, and men, plain men, became supremely important, as defenders of their imperilled homes. In this swift return to primitive conditions, primitive qualities reasserted their value. France, Belgium, England called to their sons for succour, and the arms of these men

Women and War

were strengthened because they had
women to protect.

A casual study of newspapers before
and after the proclamation of war is
profoundly instructive. Even the illustrated papers and periodicals tell their
tale, and spare us the printed page. Pictures of recruits in place of club-women.
Pictures of camps in place of convention halls. Pictures of Red Cross nurses
bending over hospital beds, in place of
militants raiding Buckingham Palace.
Pictures of peaceful ladies sewing and
knitting for soldiers, in place of formi-
dable committees baiting Mr. Wilson,
or pursuing the more elusive Mr. Asquith. Pictures of pitying young girls
handing cups of broth and the ever-wel-
come cigarettes to weary volunteers, in
place of suffragists haranguing the mob
of Hyde Park. Never was there such a
noteworthy illustration of Scott's archaic
line, —

"O woman! in our hours of ease."

Counter-Currents

Never did the simplicities of life so triumphantly efface its complexities.

As the war deepened, and the tale of its devastations and brutalities robbed even the saddened onlooker of all gladness in life, it was natural that women, while faithful to their rôle of ministering angels, should mingle blame with pity. It was also natural, though less pardonable, that their censure should be of that vague order which holds everybody responsible for what somebody has done. Perhaps it was even natural that, confident in their own unproved wisdom and untried efficiency, they should believe and say that, had women shared the control of civilized governments, the world would now be at peace.

Here we enter the realms of pure conjecture, — realms in which everything can be asserted and denied, nothing proved or disproved. It may be that when women become voters, legislators,

Women and War

and officeholders, they will do the better work for this profound and touching belief in their own perfectibility. Or it may be that a perilous self-confidence will — until corrected by experience — lead them astray. These speculations would be of small concern, were it not that the claim to moral superiority, which women advance without a blush, disposes many of them to ignore the hard conditions under which men struggle, and fail, and struggle again. It narrows their outlook, confuses their judgment, and cheapens their point of view.

When a prominent American feminist said smartly that war is the hysteria of men, she betrayed that lamentable lack of perspective which ignorance can only partly excuse. The heartless shallowness of such a speech commended it to many hearers; but of all generalizations it is the least legitimate. There was as little hysteria in the well-ordered, deeply laid plans of Germany as there was in the heroic defence of France and Belgium, or in the slow awakening of England, who took a deal of rousing from her sleep. "Most women," says Mr. Martin Chaloner, "regard politics as a kind of foolishness that men play at." But the campaign in Belgium is not to be classed as "foolishness" or "hysteria." The attack was a crime past all forgiveness; the defence was one of flawless valour. If it be hysterical to prize home and country more than life, then we must re-write that temperate old axiom which has swayed men's souls for centuries: "Dulce et decorum est pro patria mori."

Mrs. Pethick Lawrence, an English-woman and an advanced feminist, has devoted many busy months to persuading American women that the incapacity of men to rule the world is abundantly proven by the present state of Europe, and that the downfall of all that civilization has held dear is due to their arrogant rejection of feminine advice. Women,

Women and War

she asserts, are the "natural custodians
of the human race"; they have for years
"sought to find entrance into the councils of the human commonwealth, in
order that they might there represent the
supreme issue of race-preservation and
development"; now at last their hands
must be free "to build up a surer and
safer structure of humanity."

"To-day it is for men to stand down,
and for the women whom they have be-
littled to take the seat of judgment. No
picture, however overdrawn, of woman's
ignorance, error, or folly could exceed in
fantastic yet tragic horror the spectacle
which male governments are furnishing
history to-day. The foundation of the
structure of civilization which they have
erected in Europe has proved rotten.
The edifice, seemingly so secure, has
collapsed. The failure of male statecraft
in Europe is complete."

This is a bitter indictment, and one not
to be lightly disregarded. But its terms

are too general to support an argument.
What could the women of Belgium and
the women of France have done to save
their countries from invasion? When we
are told that "the woman-movement and
war cannot flourish together," and that
we should never have witnessed this
"campaign of race-suicide," had women
been justly represented, we have no answer to make, because a denial would be
as hypothetical as is the assertion. But
when Mrs. Lawrence ventures to call the
war "a great dog-fight," caused by an
"obsession of materialism," we recognize
a smallness of vision and coarseness of
speech incompatible with clear thinking,
or with that distinction of mind which
commands attention and respect. If this
militant pacifist sees in the conduct of
England and in the conduct of France
only the greed of two dogs, squabbling
with Germany over a bone, which apparently belongs to none of them, we can
but hope she is not expressing the views,

Women and War

or illustrating the knowledge of her countrywomen.

Great events, however lamentable, must be looked at greatly. There is much to be commended in the peace platform endorsed by the suffragists in Washington, January, 1915. There is everything to be hoped for in the sane and just settlement of national disputes by an international tribunal, which might advantageously include women representatives. The decisions of such a tribunal must, however, be supported by something stronger than sentiment, which has proved singularly inefficacious in the past. It is well that men and women should work hand in hand for peace and for prosperity ; but it is not well that women should invite themselves to "take the seat of judgment" ; or that they should be complacently sure that their arguments would have prevailed, when similar arguments, advanced by men, have been unheeded.

What, after all, is the line of reasoning

Counter-Currents

which Mrs. Lawrence sincerely believes would have swayed the councils of the nations? After assuring us that "the woman's movement is spiritual and religious, founded on the belief that human life is sacred," she continues : " As mothers, women would have impressed upon men the cost of human replenishment; as chancellors of the family exchequer, their influence would have been felt in forcing legislatures to recognize the direct relation between the plenteousness of the food-supply, endangered and restricted by war, and the health and growth of the rising generation."

If this is not "an obsession of materialism," where shall we look for such a quality? The world has not waited until now to learn the cost of war. It was one of the stock arguments urged upon every conference at The Hague. It was one of the indubitable facts upon which we all relied to keep the nations at peace. And it has failed us, as materialism always does fail

Women and War

us in every great national crisis. Germany knows the cost of war, but she is out for conquest, and the spoils of conquest. She recalls with pleasure the two hundred million pounds extorted from France in 1871, she hopes this time to "bleed her white" (Bismarck's cruel phrase is a compendium of Prussian policy), she dangles before German eyes the promise of indemnities which will make good all losses, and she enjoys a foretaste of bliss by levying ruinous fines upon French and Flemish towns which have tasted the utmost bitterness of defeat. France knows the cost of war, and is ill prepared to pay it; but her alternative is yielding her soil, and all she holds sacred and dear, to a ruthless invader. Even a nation of Quakers, or, we hope, a nation with women in "the seat of judgment," would reject submission on such terms. England knows the cost of war, but she also knows the cost of German supremacy. She is at last aware that her national life is at stake.

Counter-Currents

She must fight to preserve it, or sink into insignificance, — her glorious past as much a thing of memory as is the past of Rome.

For all these reasons the nations are spending their money on armaments, and spilling their blood on the battlefield. The sacredness of life is being violated; but is it life, or is it the moral worth of life, which we hold sacred? Life is a thing given us for a few years. Its only value lies in the use we make of it. Lose it we must, and very soon. But honour and duty are for all time. Why do we see a "soldiers' monument" in nearly every town of every state which fought for the Union? Not because these men lived, but because they died. What must it have cost Mr. Lincoln, whose heart was big enough for much suffering, to order from an exhausted country the last draft of half a million men! And why does an ingenious writer, like Mr. G. Lowes Dickinson, cudgel his brain to find abstract causes

Women and War

for war? The concrete causes which have come within the personal experiences of most of us will answer our rational questionings.

If it were possible that the women of all nations could ever be brought to think and feel alike, — a miracle of unity never vouchsafed to men, — then they might run the world harmoniously. If, for example, a Frau Professor Treitschke, a Frau General von Bernhardi, and the more august spouse of the Chancellor Bethmann-Hollweg had succeeded in talking down their martial husbands, and persuading Germany that her duty was to breed in peace within her own frontier, then a Madame Poincaré, a Madame Joffre, a Mrs. Asquith, a Lady Kitchener would have had no difficulty in holding back France and England from war. If the Kaiserin were an autocratic "peacelady," ruling her "war-lord" into submission, then the Queen of England and the Queen of Belgium might be drinking tea with her to-day. But unless the good Teuton women had kept their men at home, how could the good French and Belgian women have warded off attack? And would the good British women have said, "We are safe for a little while. Let us stand cringing by, and see injustice done"?

The "Woman's Journal" wrote a year ago to a number of more or less distinguished people, and asked them if they thought that woman suffrage would abolish, or would lessen war. As none of these more or less distinguished people had any data upon which to build an opinion, their answers were interesting, only as expressing personal views of a singularly untrammelled order. There were those who believed that the Spartan mother stood for an undying type, and there were those who believed that she had been finally and happily superseded. Miss Jane Addams wrote that more women than men "recognize the folly and wickedness of

Women and War

war," — an easy generalization. Dr. Stephen S. Wise, an unblinking enthusiast,
held that one great gain will follow the
tragic conditions of to-day. We shall see
the end of "man-made government."
" World peace " and " world welfare "
will come with woman's rule. Miss Mary
Johnston was of the opinion that "war
has still a fascination for most men," but
that few women feel its seduction.

Miss Johnston's view is the only one
which invites comment, because it is
shared by a great many women who have
not her excuse. "The Long Roll" and
"Cease Firing" are pretty grim pictures
of battle, but there is a heroic quality
about both books; while in that jolly,
chivalrous, piratical romance, " To Have
and to Hold," combat follows combat
with dizzy speed and splendour. Miss
Johnston's heroes take so kindly to fighting that she naturally believes in the impelling power of war; but, outside the
covers of a historical novel, the martial

Counter-Currents

instinct is not a common one. It exists, and it crops up where we least expect to find it, — in professors of political economy, in doctors who have spent their existence keeping people alive, and in clergymen who preach the religion of the meek. But it is too rare to be a controlling force, and it had little or no place in the hearts of the thousands of men who were marched to their deaths on the battlefields of Poland and Flanders.

It was not the fascination of war that brought the Tyrolean and Bavarian peasants down from their mountain farms. What did these men know or care about Belgrade, or Prussia's wide ambitions? What to them was "the fate-appointed world-task of Germany, under the sacred dynasty of the Hohenzollern"? They were summoned, and they obeyed the summons. If the women who talk so glibly about the pleasure men take in fighting had seen these conscripts saying good-bye to

Women and War

their wives and children, and marching off, grave, silent, sad, they might revise their notions of military enthusiasm. Madame Rosika Schwimmer of Budapest said before a convention in Nashville that, had her countrywomen been represented in the government, there would have been no war. The remark was received with an enthusiasm which indicates some ignorance concerning Hungary's position and power. But did Madame Schwimmer's audience believe that *all* her countrywomen hated war, and *all* her countrymen desired it? And how many of these countrymen, did Nashville think, had any choice in the matter?

When we turn from the attack to the defence, from the assailants to the assailed, we find as little room for "fascination" as for peace. The war was carried with incredible vigour and speed to the thresholds of French and Belgian homes. It was not precisely a tournament, in which battle-loving knights rode prancing and curveting to the fray. It was the older and simpler story of a land swept by invasion, and of men fighting and dying for all that belonged to them on earth. Do the American women who prate about the wrong done to womanhood by war ever reflect that it is for wife and child, as well as for home and country, that men are bound to die? What history do they read which does not teach them this truth, which does not tell it over and over again, to interpret the story of the nations?

In the town of Lexington, Massachusetts, where was shed the first blood spilled in the Revolution, there slept peacefully on the morning of April 19, 1775, a young man named Jonathan Harrington. To him in the early dawn came his widowed mother, who aroused him, saying, "Jonathan, Jonathan, wake up! The Regulars are coming, and something must be done." The some-

Women and War

thing to be done was plain to this young American, who had never fought, nor seen fighting, in his life. He rose, dressed, took his musket, joined the little group of townsmen on the Common, and fell before the first volley fired by the British soldiers. His wife (he had been married less than a year) ran to the door. He crawled across the Common, bleeding heavily, and died on his threshold at her feet.

It is a very simple incident, and it holds all the elements which make for national life. A cause to support, a man to support it, a woman to call for help when the supreme moment comes. Something like it must have happened over and over again in the blood-soaked land of Belgium. Yet we find women to-day talking and writing as if none of their sex had anything at stake in the defence of their violated homes, as if they had no sacred rights bound up with the sacred rights of men. The National American

Counter-Currents

Woman Suffrage Association sent an appeal to organized suffragists all over the world, urging them to "arise in protest, and show war-crazed men that between the contending armies there stand thousands of women and children who are the innocent victims of man's unbridled ambitions."

There was no word in this appeal to indicate that any nobler — and humbler — sentiment than unbridled ambition (which, after all, is for the very few) animates the soldier's heart. There was no distinction drawn between aggressive and defensive warfare. There was no hint that men bear their full share of the sufferings caused by war. The assumption that women endure all the pain is in accordance with the assumption that men enjoy all the pleasure. To write as though battle were a game, played by men at the expense of women, is childish and irrational. We Americans are happily spared the sight of mangled sol-

Women and War

diers lying in undreamed-of agony on
the frozen field. We do not see the
ghastly ambulance trains jolting along
with their load of broken, tortured men;
or the hospitals where these wrecks are
nursed back to some poor remnant of
life, or escape through the merciful gates
of death. But we might read of these
things; we might visualize them in moments of comfortable leisure, and take
shame to our souls at the platform eloquence which so readily assumes that
the sorrows of war are hidden in women's hearts, that the burdens of war are
laid upon women's shoulders, that women are sacrificed in their helplessness
to the hatred and the ambitions, the
greed and the glory of men.

If by any chance a word of regret is expressed for the soldier who dies for his
country, it is always because he is the
son of his mother, or the husband of his
wife, or the father of his child. He is
never permitted an entity of his own. It

is curious that the same women who
clamour for a recognition of their individual freedom should assume these property rights in men. Dr. Anna Shaw has
commented sarcastically upon a habit
(one of many bad habits) which she has
observed in the unregenerate sex. They
speak of their womenkind in terms of relationship ; they use the possessive case.
They say, " my wife," " my sister," " my
daughter," " my mother," " my aunt,"
instead of " Jane," " Susan," " Mary
Ann," "Mrs. Smith," " Miss Jones." Apparently Dr. Shaw does not hear women
say, " my husband," " my brother," " my
son," " my father," " my uncle " ; or, if
she does, this sounds less feudal in her
ears. Advanced feminists have protested
against the custom of " branding a woman at marriage with her husband's
name." Even the convenience of such an
arrangement fails to excuse its arrogance.

Yet we are bidden to protest against

Women and War

the wickedness of all war, not because men die, but because wives are widowed; not because men slay, but because mothers are childless; not because men do evil, or suffer wrong, but because, in either case, women share the consequences. For the sake of these women, war must cease, is the cry; as though the vast majority of men would not be glad enough to be rid of war for their own sake. They do not covet loss of income and destruction of property. They do not gladly aspire to an armless or legless future. Not one of them really wants a shattered thigh, or a bullet in his abdomen. And, in addition to these (perhaps selfish) considerations, we might do them the justice to remember that they are not destitute of natural affection for their wives and children; but that, on the contrary, the safeguarding of the family is, and has always been, a powerful factor in war. It lent a desperate courage to the Belgian soldier who saw his

Counter-Currents

home destroyed; it nerved the arm of the French soldier who knew his home in peril. The killing of the first women and children at Scarborough sent a host of tardy volunteers into the British army. Such indiscriminate slaughter, though it represents a negligible loss to a nation, is about the only thing on earth which the least valiant men cannot stomach.

> "The Turk, not squeamish as a rule,
> No special glee betrayed,
> And even Mr. Bernard Shaw
> Failed to commend the raid."

The Lusitania children, lying in pitiful rows to await identification in Queenstown, little meek and sodden corpses buffeted out of comeliness by the waves, awoke in the hearts of the men who looked at them a passion of anger and hate which life is too short to appease. The brutal shooting of an English nurse was followed by an illogical rush of young Englishmen to the colours. And the mere

Women and War

fact that scores of writers, commenting on Edith Cavell's death, harkened back to the beheading of Alice Lisle, proves the imperishable nature of the infamy attached to a deed, which to Judge Jeffreys, as to General Baron von Bissing, seemed the most reasonable thing in the world.

The outbreak of the war was seized upon as a strong argument for diametrically opposite views. A small and hardy minority kicked up its heels and shouted, "Women cannot fight. Why should they control a land they are powerless to defend?" A large and sentimental majority lifted up its eyes to Heaven, and answered, "If women had possessed their rights, all would now be smiling and at peace." And neither of these contending factions took any trouble to ascertain and understand the rights and wrongs of the conflict. People who pin their faith to a catchword never feel the necessity of understanding anything.

Counter-Currents

Here, for example, is a violent pacifist in the "Woman's Journal," who, to the oft-repeated assertion that women, when they have the vote, "will compel governments to settle their disputes before an international court of arbitration," adds this unwarranted statement : "The women of the world have no quarrel with one another. They do not care whether or not Austria maintains its power over the Balkan States; whether or not France obtains revenge for the defeats of 1870; whether Germany or England gains supremacy in the world market."

This good lady does not seem to know what happened in August, 1914. France did not proclaim war upon Germany. Germany proclaimed war upon France. France did not attack, — for revenge, or for any other motive. She was attacked, and has been fighting ever since with her back to the wall in defence of her own soil.

Women and War

It is possible for an American woman to have no quarrel with any one, no knowledge of what Europe is quarrelling about, and no human concern as to which nations win. But she should not think, and she certainly should not say, that the women of the warring lands are equally ignorant, and equally unconcerned. To the Serbian woman the freedom of Serbia is a precious thing. The French woman cares with her whole soul for the preservation of France. The Belgian woman can hardly be indifferent to the ultimate fate of Belgium. It is even possible that the English and German women are not prepared to clasp one another's hands and say, "We are sisters, and it matters nothing to us whether England or Germany wins." The pitfall of the feminist is the belief that the interests of men and women can ever be severed; that what brings suffering to the one can leave the other unscathed.

What are the qualities demanded of

women in every great national crisis?
First of all, intelligence. They should
have some accurate knowledge of what
has happened, some clear understanding of the events they so glibly discuss.
There are documents in plenty to en-
lighten them. Those tense summer
months in which the war was nursed in
secrecy, are now no longer secret. We
know where the bantling was cradled,
we know what ambitions speeded it on
its evil way, and we have watched every
step of its progress. To condemn all Europe in terms of easy reprobation, to
clamour for peace without recognition
of justice, is but inconsequent chatter.
It leaves vital issues untouched, and
rational minds unmoved. The sternest
words uttered since the beginning of the
war were spoken by the London "Tab-
let," in reprobation of those American
peace-mongers who could not be brought
to understand that the hope of the Eng-
lishwoman's heart is that the man whom

she has lost, — husband, son, or brother, — should not have died in vain.

Next to intelligence, a woman's most valuable asset is a reasonable modesty. She is terribly hampered by a conviction of her own goodness. It gets in her way at every step, clouding her naturally clear perceptions, and clogging her naturally keen conscientiousness. She is wrong in assuming with Miss Addams that she feels a "peculiar moral passion of revolt against both the cruelty and the waste of war." She is wrong in assuming with Madame Schwimmer that she "supplants physical courage with moral courage," when she calls noisily for peace. There are men in plenty who feel the moral passion of revolt quite as keenly as do the most sensitive of women ; but who also feel the moral responsibility of defending the safety of their country, the sacredness of their homes. The moral courage demanded of every soldier is fully as great as the physical courage, at which women dare to sneer. It is not a light thing to give up life, — "Greater love hath no man than this, that he lay down his life for his friends;" — yet death is the least of the horrors which soldiers daily face.

The third and most vital thing asked of women in these dread days is self-sacrifice. They must give their share of help, they must bear their share of sorrow. They cannot dignify their reluctance to do this by calling it moral revolt, or moral courage, or any other high-sounding name. They cannot claim for themselves a loftier virtue on the score of their lower hardihood. Civic morality consists in putting the good of the state above the good of the individual. It has no other test. If women are, as they say, responsible for the conservation of human life, they should hold themselves responsible for the ennobling of human life, for the cherishing of some finer instinct than that of self-preservation. On

Women and War

the body of a young French lieutenant who was killed at Vermelles, there was found a letter to his wife, which contained this pregnant sentence: "Promise not to begrudge me to France, if she takes me altogether." These few words are an epitome of patriotism. Husband and wife gave to their country all they had to give; the one his life, the other her love; and both knew that there is something better than human life and love.

In the genial reign of Henry the Eighth, a docile Parliament passed, at the desire of the King, an "Act to abolish Diversity of Opinion." President Wilson, less despotic, has recommended something of the same order as a mental process, a soul-smothering, harmony-preserving, intellectual anodyne. It is called neutrality, and if it has failed to save us from shameful insults and repeated wrongs, it has kept us fairly quiet under provocation. The only authorized outlet for our emotions has been a prayer (conditions

not mentioned) for peace. Because we
have schooled ourselves to witness injustice — and occasionally suffer it — without undue resentment, and without re-
prisal, our reward in money has been very
great; and we have kept on terms with
our own souls by giving back to deso-
late Europe a little of the wealth we
drew from her. Our position has always
been a tenable one, and no nation has
had any ground on which to censure us;
but we have found in it scant encouragement for self-esteem. Even the flowers
of domestic oratory, the oft-repeated assertion that our prudence and our wealth
make us respected on earth, and blessed
in the sight of Heaven, fail to quicken
our sad hearts. For, from over the sea,
comes a cry which sounds like the echo of
words with which we were once familiar,
of which we were once proud. "With
firmness in the right, as God gives us to
see the right, let us strive on to finish the
work we are in."

Women and War

This is the potent voice of humanity, never to be silenced while men stay men. The "work" was bloody work; brother slaying brother on the battlefield. The women of the North and the women of the South bore their share of sorrow. They did not assert that they were victims of men's unbridled ambition, and they never intimated to one another that the final victory was to them a matter of unconcern. Theirs was the "solemn pride" of sacrifice; and that fine phrase, dedicated by Mr. Lincoln to the woman who had sent five sons to the conflict, is applicable to thousands of mothers to-day. The writer knows a young Frenchman who, when the war broke out, had lived for some years in this country, and hoped to make it his permanent home. To him his mother wrote: "My son, your two brothers are at the front. Are you not coming back to fight for France?" The lad had not meant to go. Perhaps he coveted safety. Perhaps he held life

Counter-Currents

(his life) to be a sacred thing. Perhaps he thought to comfort his mother's old age. But when that letter came, he sailed on the next steamer. It was a summons that few men, and certainly no Frenchman, could deny.

When the women of France refused to participate in the International Congress of Women at The Hague, they defined their position in a document so dignified, so lucid, and so logical, that it deserves to be handed down to future ages as an illustration of inspired common sense lifted to the heights of heroism. Let no one who reads it ever deny that women are capable of clear thinking, of sane and balanced judgment. In contrast to the vague and formless peace-talk which came floating over to us from Holland, and has been re-echoed ever since; talk which starting from no definite premises has reached no just conclusions, the clear utterances of these French women rang with insistent exactitude. They rejected all sentimental abstractions, and presented in a concrete form the circumstances which had pushed France into the conflict, and which held her still at bay. " It were treason to think of peace, until that peace can consecrate the principles of right."

The rationality of the French mind, the essentially practical nature of the French genius, are responsible for the form of this historic document; but back of the form lies the spirit, and the spirit is one of sustained self-sacrifice. "To-day it is with pride we wear our weeds; it is with gratitude that we perpetuate the memory of our dead." At a time when every franc could buy some sorely needed supply, when every hour could be filled with some sorely needed service, sensible Frenchwomen refused to spend both money and time in journeying to The Hague for the dear delights of talking. But deeper than their reluctance to do a wasteful thing was their reluctance to do a treasonable thing, to put the comforts of peace above the sacrifices entailed by war, to refuse by word or deed their share of a common burden.

It is absurd to suppose that these brave and suffering women do not feel a moral revolt against the cruelty and the waste of war quite as sharply as does Miss Addams, or any Hague delegate, or any one of Mr. Ford's tourists. The "basic foundation of home and of peaceful industry" is as dear to them as to the American women who talk so much about it. As a matter of fact, it is their devotion which holds together the shattered homes of France, their industry which preserves economic safety, and gives food and shelter to the destitute. And through terrible months of pain and privation, we have heard from the lips of Frenchwomen no wild and weak complaints. Never once have they assumed that they were better and nobler than their husbands and sons who died for the needs of France.

When the late Justice Brewer said

Women and War

that "since the beginning of days" women have been opposed to bloodshed, we wondered — without doubting the truth of his assertion — how he came to find it out. Certainly not from the pages of history, which afford little or no evidence on the subject. This may be one reason why feminists are protesting stoutly against the way in which history has been written, its indiscreet revelations, its disconcerting silences. At a meeting of the Women's Political Union in New York, October, 1914, it was boldly urged that history should be re-written on a peace basis; less emphasis placed upon nationalism, less space devoted to wars. At a meeting of the National Municipal League in Baltimore the same year, it was urged that history should be re-written on a feminine basis; less emphasis placed upon men, less space devoted to their achievements. One revolutionist complained with exceeding bitterness that President

Counter-Currents

Wilson hardly makes mention of women in his five volumes of American history. The "knell" of that kind of narrative, she intimated, had "rung."

The historian of the future will find his task pleasantly simplified. He will be a little like two young Americans whom I once met scampering blithely over southern Europe, and to whom I ventured to say that they covered their ground quickly. "No trouble about that," answered one of them. "We draw the line at churches and galleries, and there's nothing left to see." So, too, the chronicler who eliminates men and war from his pages can move swiftly down the centuries. Even an earnest effort to minimize these factors suggests that blight of my girlhood, Miss Strickland, who forever strove to withdraw her wandering attention from warrior and statesman, and fix it on the trousseau of a queen.

History is, and has always been trammelled by facts. It may ignore some

Women and War

and deny others ; but it cannot accom-
modate itself unreservedly to theories ;
it cannot be stripped of things evidenced
in favour of things surmised. Perhaps
instead of asking to have it remodelled
in our behalf, we women might take the
trouble to read it as it is ; dominated by
men, disfigured by conflict, but not altogether ignoble or unprofitable, and
always very enlightening. We might
learn from it, for example, that war may
be wicked, and war may be justifiable;
that wife and child, far from being unconsidered trifles, have nerved men's
arms to strike ; and that when home,
country, freedom and justice are at
stake, " it were treason to think of peace,
until that peace can consecrate the principles of right."

The Repeal of Reticence

THERE is nothing new about the Seven Deadly Sins. They are as old as humanity. There is nothing mysterious about them. They are easier to understand than the Cardinal Virtues. Nor have they dwelt apart in secret places ; but, on the contrary, have presented themselves, undisguised and unabashed, in every corner of the world, and in every epoch of recorded history. Why then do so many men and women talk and write as if they had just discovered these ancient associates of mankind? Why do they press upon our reluctant notice the result of their researches? Why this fresh enthusiasm in dealing with a foul subject? Why this relentless determination to make us intimately acquainted with matters of which a casual knowledge would suffice?

136

The Repeal of Reticence

Above all, why should our self-appointed instructors assume that because we do not chatter about a thing, we have never heard of it? The well-ordered mind knows the value, no less than the charm, of reticence. The fruit of the tree of knowledge, which is now recommended as nourishing for childhood, strengthening for youth, and highly restorative for old age, falls ripe from its stem ; but those who have eaten with sobriety find no need to discuss the processes of digestion. Human experience is very, very old. It is our surest monitor, our safest guide. To ignore it crudely is the error of those ardent but uninstructed missionaries who have lightly undertaken the re-building of the social world.

Therefore it is that the public is being daily instructed concerning matters which it was once assumed to know, and which, as a matter of fact, it has always known. When "The Lure" was played three years ago at the Maxine Elliott Theatre in New York, the redoubtable Mrs. Pankhurst arose in Mrs. Belmont's box, and, unsolicited, informed the audience that it was the truth which was being nakedly presented to them, and that as truth it should be taken to heart. Now, it is probable that the audience — adult men and women — knew as much about the situations developed in "The Lure" as did Mrs. Pankhurst. It is possible that some of them knew more, and could have given her points. But whatever may be the standard of morality, the standard of taste (and taste is a guardian of morality) must be curiously lowered, when a woman spectator at an indecent play commends its indecencies to the careful consideration of the audience. Even the absurdity of the proceeding fails to win pardon for its grossness.

It is not so much the nature of the advice showered upon us to which we reasonably object, but the fact that a

The Repeal of Reticence

great deal of it is given in the wrong
way, at the wrong time, by the wrong
people. Who made Mrs. Pankhurst our
nursery governess, and put us in *her*
hands for schooling? We might safely
laugh at and ignore these unsolicited
exhortations, were it not that the crude
detailing of matters offensive to modesty
is as hurtful to the young as it is weari-
some to the old. Does it never occur to
the women, who are now engaged in
telling the world what the world has
known since the days of Nineveh, that
more legitimate, and, on the whole, more
enlightened avenues exist for the distri-
bution of such knowledge?

> "Are there no clinics at our gates,
> Nor any doctors in the land?"

The "Conspiracy of Silence" is broken.
Of that no one can doubt. The phrase
may be suffered to lapse into oblivion.
In its day it was a menace, and few of
us would now advocate the deliberate

Counter-Currents

ignoring of things not to be denied. Few of us would care to see the rising generation as uninstructed in natural laws as we were, as adrift amid the unintelligible, or partly intelligible things of life. But surely the breaking of silence need not imply the opening of the floodgates of speech. It was never meant by those who first cautiously advised a clearer understanding of sexual relations and hygienic laws that everybody should chatter freely respecting these grave issues; that teachers, lecturers, novelists, story-writers, militants, dramatists, and social workers should copiously impart all they know, or assume they know, to the world. The lack of restraint, the lack of balance, the lack of soberness and common sense were never more apparent than in the obsession of sex, which has set us all a-babbling about matters once excluded from the amenities of conversation.

Knowledge is the cry. Crude, undigested knowledge, without limit and

The Repeal of Reticence

without reserve. Give it to boys, give
it to girls, give it to children. No other
force is taken into account by the vision-
aries who — in defiance, or in ignorance,
of history — believe that evil understood
is evil conquered. "The menace of degradation and destruction can be checked
only by the dissemination of knowledge
on the subject of sex-physiology and
hygiene," writes an enthusiast in the
"Forum," calling our attention to the
methods which have been employed by
some public schools, noticeably the Polytechnic High School of Los Angeles, for
the instruction of students ; and urging
that similar lectures be given to boys
and girls in the grammar schools. It is
noticeable that while a woman doctor
was employed to lecture to the girl students of the Polytechnic, a "science
man" was chosen by preference for the
boys. Doctors are proverbially reticent,
— except, indeed, on the stage, where
they prattle of all they know ; but a

Counter-Currents

"science man" — as distinct from a man of science — may be trusted, if he be young and ardent, to conceal little or nothing from his hearers. The lectures were obligatory for the boys, but optional for the girls, whose inquisitiveness could be relied upon. "The universal eagerness of under-classmen to reach the serene upper heights" (I quote the language of the "Forum") "gave the younger girls increased interest in the advanced lectures, if, indeed, a girl's natural curiosity regarding these vital facts needs any stimulus."

Perhaps it does not, but I am disposed to think it receives a strong artificial stimulus from instructors whose minds are unduly engrossed with sexual problems, and that this artificial stimulus is a menace rather than a safeguard. We hear too much about the thirst for knowledge from people keen to quench it. Dr. Edward L. Keyes advocates the teaching of sex-hygiene to children, because

The Repeal of Reticence

he thinks it is the kind of information that children are eagerly seeking. "What is this topic," he asks, "that all these little ones are questioning over, mulling over, fidgeting over, imagining over, worrying over? Ask your own memories."

I do ask my memory in vain for the answer Dr. Keyes anticipates. A child's life is so full, and everything that enters it seems of supreme importance. I fidgeted over my hair, which would not curl. I worried over my examples, which never came out right. I mulled (though unacquainted with the word) over every piece of sewing put into my incapable fingers, which could not be trained to hold a needle. I imagined I was stolen by brigands, and became — by virtue of beauty and intelligence — spouse of a patriotic outlaw in a frontierless land. I asked artless questions which brought me into discredit with my teachers, as, for example, who "massacred" St. Bar-

tholomew. But vital facts, the great laws
of propagation, were matters of but
casual concern, crowded out of my life,
and out of my companions' lives (in a
convent boarding-school) by the more
stirring happenings of every day. How
could we fidget over obstetrics when we
were learning to skate, and our very
dreams were a medley of ice and bumps?
How could we worry over "natural
laws" in the face of a tyrannical inter-
dict which lessened our chances of breaking our necks by forbidding us to coast
down a hill covered with trees? The
children to be pitied, the children whose
minds become infected with unwhole-
some curiosity, are those who lack cheerful recreation, religious teaching, and the
fine corrective of work. A playground
or a swimming-pool will do more to keep
them mentally and morally sound than
scores of lectures upon sex-hygiene.

The point of view of the older generation was not altogether the futile thing

The Repeal of Reticence

it seems to the progressive of to-day. It assumed that children brought up in honour and goodness, children disciplined into some measure of self-restraint, and taught very plainly the difference between right and wrong in matters childish and seasonable, were in no supreme danger from the gradual and somewhat haphazard expansion of knowledge. It unconsciously reversed the adage, "Forewarned, forearmed," into " Forearmed, forewarned"; paying more heed to the arming than to the warning. It held that the workingman was able to rear his children in decency. The word degradation was not so frequently coupled with poverty as it is now. Nor was it anybody's business in those simple days to impress upon the poor the wretchedness of their estate.

If knowledge alone could save us from sin, the salvation of the world would be easy work. If by demonstrating the injuriousness of evil, we could insure the acceptance of good, a little logic would redeem mankind. But the laying of the foundation of law and order in the mind, the building up of character which will be strong enough to reject both folly and vice, — this is no facile task.

The justifiable reliance placed by our fathers upon religion and discipline has given place to a reliance upon understanding. It is assumed that youth will abstain from wrong-doing, if only the physical consequences of wrong-doing are made sufficiently clear. There are those who believe that a regard for future generations is a powerful deterrent from immorality, that boys and girls can be so interested in the quality of the baby to be born in 1990 that they will master their wayward impulses for its sake. What does not seem to occur to us is that this deep sense of obligation to ourselves and to our fellow creatures is the fruit of self-control. A course of lectures will not instil self-control into the

The Repeal of Reticence

human heart. It is born of childish virtues acquired in childhood, youthful virtues acquired in youth, and a wholesome
preoccupation with the activities of life
which gives young people something to
think about besides the sexual relations
which are pressed so relentlessly upon
their attention.

The world is wide, and a great deal is
happening in it. I do not plead for ignorance, but for the gradual and harmonious broadening of the field of knowledge,
and for a more careful consideration of
ways and means. There are subjects
which may be taught in class, and subjects which commend themselves to individual teaching. There are topics which
admit of *plein-air* handling, and topics
which civilized man, as apart from his
artless brother of the jungles, has veiled
with reticence. There are truths which
may be, and should be, privately imparted by a father, a mother, a family
doctor, or an experienced teacher; but

Counter-Currents

which young people cannot advantageously acquire from the platform, the stage, the moving-picture gallery, the novel, or the ubiquitous monthly magazine.

Yet all these sources of information are competing with one another as to which shall tell us most. All of them have missions, and all the missions are alike. We are gravely assured that the drama has awakened to a high and holy duty, that it has a "serious call," in obedience to which it has turned the stage into a clinic for the diagnosing of disease, and into a self-authorized commission for the intimate study of vice. It advertises itself as "battling with the evils of the age," — which are the evils of every age, — and its method of warfare is to exploit the sins of the sensual for the edification of the virtuous, to rake up the dunghills with the avowed purpose of finding a jewel. The doors of the brothel have been flung hospitably

The Repeal of Reticence

open, and we have been invited to peep
and peer (always in the interests of morality) into regions which were formerly
closed to the uninitiated. It has been discovered that situations, once the exclusive
property of the police courts, make valuable third acts, or can be usefully employed in curtain-lifters, unclean and un-
dramatic, but which claim to "tell their
story so clearly that the daring is lost in
the splendid moral lesson conveyed."
Familiarity with vice (which an old-fash-
ioned but not inexperienced moralist
like Pope held to be a perilous thing) is
advocated as a safeguard, especially for
the young and ardent. The lowering of
our standard of taste, the deadening of
our finer sensibilities, are matters of no
moment to dramatist or to manager.
They have other interests at stake.

For depravity is a valuable asset when
presented to the consideration of the un-
depraved. It has coined money for the
proprietors of moving-pictures, who for

the past few years have been sending shows with attractive titles about "White Slaves," and "Outcasts," and "Traffic in Souls," all over the country. Many of these shows claimed to be dramatizations of the reports of vice-commissioners, who have thus entered the arena of sport, and become purveyors of pleasure to the multitude. "Original," "Authentic," "Authorized," are words used freely in their advertisements. The public is assured that "care has been taken to eliminate all suggestiveness," which is in a measure true. When everything is told, there is no room left for suggestions. If you kick a man down stairs and out of the door, you may candidly say that you never suggested he should leave your house. Now and then a particularly lurid revelation is commended to us as having received the endorsement of leading feminists; and again we are driven to ask why should these ladies assume an intimate knowledge of such alien mat-

The Repeal of Reticence

ters? Why should they play the part of mentors to such an experienced Telemachus as the public?

It is hard to estimate the harm done by this persistent and crude handling of sexual vice. The peculiar childishness inherent in all moving-picture shows may possibly lessen their hurtfulness. What if the millionaires and the political bosses so depicted spend their existence in entrapping innocent young women? A single policeman of tender years, a single girl, inexperienced but resourceful, can defeat these fell conspirators, and bring them all to justice. Never were villains so helpless in a hard and virtuous world. But silliness is no sure safeguard, and to excite in youth a curiosity concerning brothels and their inmates can hardly fail of mischief. To demonstrate graphically and publicly the value of girls in such places is to familiarize them dangerously with sin. I can but hope that the little children who sit stol-

idly by their mothers' sides, and whom
the authorities of every town should exclude from all shows dealing with prostitution, are saved from defilement by the
invincible ignorance of childhood. As for
the groups of boys and young men who
compose the larger part of the audiences,
and who snigger and whisper whenever
the situations grow intense, nobody in
his senses could assert that the pictures
convey a "moral lesson" to them.

Nor is it for the conveying of lessons
that managers present these photo-plays
to the public. They are out to make
money, and they are making it. Granted
that when M. Brieux wrote "Les Ava-
riés," he purposed a stern warning to the
pleasure-loving world. No one can read
the simple and sober words with which
he prefaced the work, and doubt his absolute sincerity. Granted, though with
some misgivings, that the presentation
of "Damaged Goods" in this country —
albeit commercialized and a smart busi-

The Repeal of Reticence

ness venture — had still a moral and scientific significance. It was not primarily designed as an exploitation of vice. But to tell such a story in moving pictures is to rob it of all excuse for being told at all. To thrust such a theme grossly and vulgarly before the general public, stripping it of nobility of thought and exactitude of speech, and leaving only the dull dregs of indecency, is an uncondonable offense, — the deeper because it claims to be beneficent.

In one respect all the studies of seduction now presented so urgently to our regard are curiously alike. They all conspire to lift the burden of blame from the woman's shoulders, to free her from any sense of human responsibility. It is assumed that she plays no part in her own undoing, that she is as passive as the animal bought for vivisection, as mute and helpless in the tormentors' hands. The tissue of false sentiment woven about her has resulted in an extraordi-

Counter-Currents

nary confusion of outlook, a perilous nullification of honesty and honour.

To illustrate this point, I quote some verses which appeared in a periodical devoted to social work, a periodical with high and serious aims. I quote them reluctantly (not deeming them fit for publication), and only because it is impossible to ignore the fact that their appearance in such a paper makes them doubly and trebly reprehensible. They are entitled " The Cry to Christ of the Daughters of Shame."

" Crucified once for the sins of the world,
  O fortunate Christ!" they cry:
" With an Easter dawn in thy dying eyes,
  O happy death to die!

" But we, — we are crucified daily,
  With never an Easter morn;
But only the hell of human lust,
  And worse, — of human scorn.

" For the sins of passionless women,
  For the sins of passionate men,

The Repeal of Reticence

Daily we make atonement,
　Golgotha again and again.

"O happy Christ, who died for love,
　Judge us who die for lust.
For thou wast man, who now art God.
　Thou knowest. Thou art just."

Now apart from the offence against religion in this easy comparison between the Saviour and the woman of the streets, and apart from the deplorable offence against good taste, which might repel even the irreligious, such unqualified acquittal stands forever in the way of reform, of the judgment and common sense which make for the betterment of the world. How is it possible to awaken any healthy emotion in the hearts of sinners so smothered in sentimentality? How is it possible to make girls and young women (as yet respectable) understand not only the possibility, but the obligation of a decent life?

There would be less discussion of meretricious subjects, either in print or in conversation, were it not for the morbid sensibility which has undermined our judgment, and set our nerves a-quivering. Even a counsellor so sane and so experienced as the Reverend Honourable Edward Lyttelton, Headmaster of Eton, who has written an admirable volume on "Training of the Young in Laws of Sex," drops his tone of wholesome austerity as soon as he turns from the safeguarding of lads to the pensive consideration of women. Boys and men he esteems to be captains of their souls, but the woman is adrift on the sea of life. He does not urge her to restraint; he pleads for her to the masters of her fate. "The unhappy partners of a rich man's lust," he writes, "are beings born with the mighty power to love, and are endowed with deep and tender instincts of loyalty and motherhood. When these divine and lovely graces of character are utterly shattered and foully degraded, the man, on whom all the treasure has

The Repeal of Reticence

been lavished, tries to believe that he has made ample reparation by an annuity of fifty pounds."

This kind of sentiment is out of place in everything save eighteenth-century lyrics, which are not expected to be a guiding force in morals. A woman with "lovely graces of character" does not usually become the mistress even of a rich man. After all, there is such a thing as triumphant virtue. It has an established place in the annals and traditions, the ballads and stories of every land.

"A mayden of England, sir, never will be
The wench of a monarcke," quoth Mary Ambree.

It is like a breath of fresh air blowing away mists to hear this gay and gallant militant assert the possibilities of resistance.

Forty years ago, a writer in "Blackwood's Magazine" commented upon the amazing fact that in Hogarth's day (more than a century earlier) vignettes representing the "Rake's Progress," and the "Harlot's Progress," were painted upon fans carried by young women. "English girls," said this sober essayist, "were thus, by way of warning, made familiar with subjects now wisely withheld from their consideration."

The pendulum has swung backward since 1876. Even Hogarth, who dealt for the most part with the robust simplicities of sin, would have little to teach the rising generation of 1916. Its sources of knowledge are manifold, and astoundingly explicit. Stories minutely describing houses of ill-fame, their furniture, their food, their barred windows, their perfumed air, and the men with melancholy eyes who visit them. Novels purporting to be candid and valuable studies of degeneracy and nymphomania. Plays and protests urging stock-farm methods of breeding the human race. Papers on venereal diseases scattered broadcast through the land. Comment upon those

The Repeal of Reticence

unnatural vices which have preceded the ruin of cities and the downfall of nations, and veiled allusions to which have marked the deepest degradation of the French stage. All these horrors, which would have made honest old Hogarth turn uneasily in his grave, are offered for the defence of youth and the purifying of civilized society.

The lamentable lack of reserve is closely associated with a lamentable absence of humour. We should be saved from many evils, if we could laugh at more absurdities. We could clearly estimate the value of reform, if we were not so befuddled with the sensationalism of reformers, and so daunted by the amazing irregularity of their methods. What can be thought of a woman who goes to a household of strangers, and volunteers to instruct its members in sex-hygiene! In the case which came under my notice, the visitor chanced upon a family of spinsters, discreet, retiring, well-conducted gentle-

Counter-Currents

women, the eldest of whom was eighty, and the youngest sixty years of age. But while this circumstance added to the humour of the situation, it in no wise lessened its insolent impropriety.

The enthusiasm for birth-control has carried its advocates so fast and so far from the conventions of society that two of them have been arrested in the State of New York for circulating indecent matter through the mails, and one has been convicted on this charge. To run amuck through the formalities of civilization, and then proclaim yourself a martyr to science and the public good, is one way of acquiring notoriety. To invite the selfish and the cowardly to follow the line of least resistance is one way, and a very easy way, of ensuring popularity. Thirty years ago, Mr. Robert Louis Stevenson wrote the story of a Spanish girl, born of a decadent and perishing race, to whom comes the promise of love, and of escape from her dire surroundings.

The Repeal of Reticence

Both these boons she rejects, knowing that the line from which she springs is fit for nothing but extinction, and knowing also that lesson hard to learn, — "that pain is the choice of the magnanimous, that it is better to suffer all things, and do well." Twenty years ago, Miss Elizabeth Robins gave us her solution of a similar problem. The heroine of her novel, fully aware that she comes of a stock diseased in mind and body, and that her lover, who is near of kin, shares this inheritance, forces upon him (he is a quiescent gentleman, more than willing to be let alone) first marriage, and then suicide. We must have our hour of happiness, is her initial demand. We must pay the price, is her ultimate decision. In our day, the noble austerity commended by Mr. Stevenson, the passionate wilfulness condoned by Miss Robins, are equally out of date. The International Neo-Malthusian Bureau has easier methods to propose, and softer ways to sanction.

Counter-Currents

It is touching to hear Mr. Percy Mac-Kaye lament that "Mendelism has as yet hardly begun to influence art or popular feeling"; but he must not lose hope, — not, at least, so far as popular feeling is concerned. "Practical eugenics" is a phrase as familiar in our ears as "intensive farming." "How can we make the desirable marry one another?" asks Dr. Alexander Graham Bell, and answers his own question by affirming that every community should take a hand in the matter, giving the "support of public opinion," and the more emphatic support of "important and well-paid positions" to a choice stock of men, provided always that, "in the interests of the race," they marry and have offspring.

This is practical eugenics with a vengeance, but it is not practical business. Apart from the fact that most men and women regard marriage as a personal matter, with which their neighbours have no concern, it does not follow that the

The Repeal of Reticence

admirable and athletic young husband possesses any peculiar ability. Little runts of men are sometimes the ablest of citizens. When Nature is in a jesting mood, her best friends marvel at her blunders.

The connection between Mendelism and art is still a trifle strained. It is an alliance which Mendel himself — good abbot of Brünn working patiently in his cloister garden — failed to take into account. The field of economics is not Art's chosen playground; the imparting of scientific truths has never been her mission. Whether she deals with high and poignant emotions, or with the fears and wreckage of life, she subdues these human elements into an austere accord with her own harmonious laws. She is as remote from the crudities of the honest but uninspired reformer who dabbles in fiction and the drama, as she is remote from the shameless camp-followers of reform, for whose base ends, no less than for our instruction and betterment, the

Counter-Currents

Seven Deadly Sins have acquired their present regrettable popularity. Liberated from the unsympathetic atmosphere of the catechism, they are urged upon the weary attention of adults, embodied in the lessons of youth, and explained in words of one syllable to childhood. Yet Hogarth never designed his pictures to decorate the fans of women. Suetonius never related his "pleasant atrocities" to the boys and girls of Rome.

Popular Education

THIS is so emphatically the children's age that a good many of us are beginning to thank God we were not born in it. The little girl who said she wished she had lived in the time of Charles the Second, because then "education was much neglected," wins our sympathy and esteem. It is a doubtful privilege to have the attention of the civilized world focussed upon us both before and after birth. At the First International Eugenics Congress, held in London in the summer of 1912, an Italian delegate made the somewhat discouraging statement that the children of very young parents are more prone than others to theft; that the children of middle-aged parents are apt to be of good conduct, but of low intelligence; and that the children of elderly parents are, as a rule,

Counter-Currents

intelligent, but badly behaved. It seems
to be a trifle hard to bring the right kind
of a child into the world. Twenty-seven
is, in this eugenist's opinion, the best age
for parentage; but how bend all the com-
plicated conditions of life to meet an ar-
bitrary date; and how remain twenty-
seven long enough to insure satisfactory
results? The vast majority of babies will
have to put up with being born when
their time comes, and make the best of
it. This is the first, but by no means the
worst, disadvantage of compulsory birth;
and compulsory birth is the original evil
which scientists and philanthropists are
equally powerless to avert.

If parents do not know by this time
how to bring up their children, it is not
for lack of instruction. A few generations
ago, Solomon was the only writer on
child-study who enjoyed any vogue.
Now his precepts, the acrid fruits of experience, have been superseded by more
genial, but more importunate counsel.

Popular Education

Begirt by well-wishers, hemmed in on every side by experts who speak of "child-material" as if it were raw silk or wood-pulp, how can a little boy, born in this enlightened age, dodge the educational influences which surround him? It is hard to be dealt with as "child-material," when one is only an ordinary little boy. To be sure, "child-material" is never thrashed, as little boys were wont to be, it is not required to do what it is told, it enjoys rights and privileges of a very sacred and exalted character; but, on the other hand, it is never let alone, and to be let alone is sometimes worth all the ministrations of men and angels. The helpless, inarticulate reticence of a child is not an obstacle to be overcome, but a barrier which protects the citadel of childhood from assault.

We can break down this barrier in our zeal; and if the child will not speak, we can at least compel him to listen. He is powerless to evade any revelations

Counter-Currents

we choose to make, any facts or theories we choose to elucidate. We can teach him sex-hygiene when he is still young enough to believe that rabbits lay eggs. We can turn his work into play, and his play into work, keeping well in mind the educational value of his unconscious activities, and, by careful oversight, pervert a game of tag into a preparation for the business of life. We can amuse and interest him until he is powerless to amuse and interest himself. We can experiment with him according to the dictates of hundreds of rival authorities. He is in a measure at our mercy, though nature fights hard for him, safeguarding him with ignorance of our mode of thought, and indifference to our point of view. The opinions of twelve-year-old Bobby Smith are of more moment to ten-year-old Tommy Jones than are the opinions of Dr. and Mrs. Jones, albeit Dr. Jones is a professor of psychology, and Mrs. Jones the president of a Parents' League. The supreme

Popular Education

value of Mr. Robert Louis Stevenson's much-quoted "Lantern Bearers" lies in its incisive and sympathetic insistence upon the aloofness of the child's world, — an admittedly imperfect world which we are burning to amend, but which closed its doors upon us forever when we grew into knowledge and reason.

My own childhood lies very far away. It occurred in what I cannot help thinking a blissful period of intermission. The educational theories of the Edgeworths (evolved soberly from the educational excesses of Rousseau) had been found a trifle onerous. Parents had not the time to instruct and admonish their children all day long. As a consequence, we enjoyed a little wholesome neglect, and made the most of it. The new era of child-study and mothers' congresses lay darkling in the future. "Symbolic education," "symbolic play," were phrases all unknown. The "revolutionary discoveries" of Karl Groos had not yet

Counter-Currents

overshadowed the innocent diversions of infancy. Nobody drew scientific deductions from jackstones, or balls, or gracehoops, save only when we assailed the wealth of nations by breaking a window-pane. Nobody was even aware that the impulses which sent us speeding and kicking up our heels like young colts were "vestigial organs of the soul." Dr. G. Stanley Hall had not yet invented this happy phrase to elucidate the simplicities of play. How we grasped our "objective relationship" to our mothers without the help of bird's-nest games, I do not know. Perhaps, in the general absence of experimentation, we had more time in which to solve the artless problems of our lives. Psychologists in those days were frankly indifferent to us. They had yet to discover our enormous value in the realms of conjectural thought.

The education of my childhood was embryonic. The education of to-day is exhaustive. The fact that the school-child

Popular Education

of to-day does not seem to know any more than we knew in the dark ages, is a side issue with which I have no concern. But as I look back, I can now see plainly that the few things little girls learned were admirably adapted for one purpose, — to make us parts of a whole, which whole was the family. I do not mean that there was any expression to this effect. "Training for maternity" was not a phrase in vogue; and the short views of life, more common then than now, would have robbed it of its savour. "Training for citizenship" had, so far as we were concerned, no meaning whatsoever. A little girl was a little girl, not the future mother of the race, or the future saviour of the Republic. One thing at a time. Therefore no deep significance was attached to our possession of a doll, no concern was evinced over our future handling of a vote. If we were taught to read aloud with correctness and expression, to write notes with propriety and

grace, and to play backgammon and
whist as well as our intelligence permitted, it was in order that we should
practise these admirable accomplish-
ments for the benefit of the families of
which we were useful, and occasionally
ornamental features.

And what advantage accrued to *us*
from an education so narrowed, so il-
liberal, so manifestly unconcerned with
great social and national issues? Well,
let us admit that it had at least the qualities of its defects. It was not called training for character, but it was admittedly
training for behaviour, and the foundations of character are the acquired habits
of youth. "Habit," said the Duke of
Wellington, "is ten times nature." There
was precision in the simple belief that
the child was strengthened mentally by
mastering its lessons, and morally by
mastering its inclinations. Therefore the
old-time teacher sought to spur the pupil
on to keen and combative effort, rather

Popular Education

than to beguile him into knowledge with cunning games and lantern slides. Therefore the old-time parent set a high value on self-discipline and self-control. A happy childhood did not necessarily mean a childhood free from proudly accepted responsibility. There are few things in life so dear to girl or boy as the chance to turn to good account the splendid self-confidence of youth.

If Saint Augustine, who was punished when he was a little lad because he loved to play, could see how childish pastimes are dignified in the pedagogy of the twentieth century, he would no longer say that "playing is the business of childhood." He would know that it is the supremely important business, the crushing responsibility of the pedagogue. Nothing is too profound, nothing too subtle to be evolved from a game or a toy. We are gravely told that "the doll with its immense educational power should be carefully introduced into the schools," that "Pussy-in-the-Corner" is "an Ariadne clew to the labyrinth of experience," and that a ball, tossed to the accompaniment of a song insultingly banal, will enable a child "to hold fast one high purpose amid all the vicissitudes of time and place." If we would only make organized play a part of the school curriculum, we should have no need of camps, or drills, or military training. It is the moulder of men, the upholder of nations, the character-builder of the world.

Mr. Joseph Lee, who has written a book of five hundred pages on "Play in Education," and Mr. Henry S. Curtis, who has written a book of three hundred and fifty pages on "Education through Play," have treated their theme with profound and serious enthusiasm, which, in its turn, is surpassed by the fervid exaltation of their reviewers. These counsellors have so much that is good to urge upon us, and we are so ready to listen to their words, that they could have well

Popular Education

afforded to be more convincingly moderate. There is no real use in saying that it is play which makes the world go round, because we know it is n't. If it were, the world of the savage would go round as efficaciously as the world of the civilized man. When Mr. Lee tells us that the little boy who plays baseball "follows the ball each day further into the unexplored regions of potential character, and comes back each evening a larger moral being than he set forth," we merely catch our breath, and read on. We have known so many boys, and we are disillusioned. When Mr. Curtis points out to us that English school-boys play more and play better than any other lads, and that their teachers advocate and encourage the love of sport because it breeds "good common sense, and resourcefulness which will enable them to meet the difficulties of life," we ask ourselves doubtfully whether Englishmen do meet life's difficulties with an intelligence so keen and adjusted as to prove the potency of play. The work which is demanded of French and German school-boys would seem to English and American school-boys (to say nothing of English and American parents) cruel and excessive; yet Frenchmen and Germans are not destitute of resourcefulness, and they meet the difficulties of life with a concentration of purpose which is the wonder of the world.

Even the moderate tax which is now imposed upon the leisure and freedom of American children has been declared illegal. It is possible and praiseworthy, we are assured, to spare them all "unnatural restrictions," all uncongenial labour. There are pastimes in plenty which will impart to them information, without demanding any effort on their part. Folk-songs, and rhythmic dances, and story-telling, and observation classes, and "wholesome and helpful games," fill up a pleasant morning for little pu-

Popular Education

pils; and when they grow bigger, more stirring sports await them. Listen to Judge Lindsey's enthusiastic description of the school-room of the future, where moving pictures will take the place of books and blackboards, where no free child will be "chained to a desk" (painful phrase!), and where "progressive educators" will make merry with their pupils all the happy day.

"Mr. Edison is coming to the rescue of Tony," says Judge Lindsey. (Tony is a boy who does not like school as it is at present organized.) "He will take him away from me, and put him in a school that is not a school at all, but just one big game; — just one round of joy, of play, of gladness, of knowledge, of sunshine, warming the cells in Tony's head until they all open up as the flowers do. There will be something moving, something doing at that school all the time, just as there is when Tony goes down to the tracks to see the engines.

Counter-Currents

"When I tell him about it, Tony shouts, 'Hooray for Mr. Edison!' right in front of the battery, just as he used to say, 'To hell wid de cop.'"

Now this is an interesting exposition of the purely sentimental view of education. We have been leading up to it for years, ever since Froebel uttered his famous "Come, let us live with our children!" and here it is set down in black and white by a man who has the welfare of the young deeply at heart. Judge Lindsey sympathizes with Tony's distaste for study. He points out to us that it is hard for a boy who is "the leader of a gang" to be laughed at by less enterprising children because he cannot cipher. Yet to some of us it does not seem altogether amiss that Tony should be brought to understand the existence of other standards than those of hoodlumism. Ciphering is dull work (so, at least, I have always found it), and difficult work too; but it is hardly fair to

Popular Education

brand it as ignoble. Compared with stealing rails from a freight-car, which is Tony's alternative for school attendance, it even has a dignity of its own; and the perception of this fact may be a salutary, if mortifying lesson. Judge Lindsey's picturesque likening of our antiquated school system which compels children to sit at desks, with the antiquated Chinese custom which bound little girls' feet, lacks discernment. The underlying motives are, in these instances, measurably different, the processes are dissimilar, the results have points of variance.

Nobody doubts that all our Tonys, rich and poor, lawless and law-abiding, would much prefer a school that is not a school at all, "but just one big game"; nobody doubts that a great deal of desultory information may be acquired from films. But desultory information is not, and never can be, a substitute for education; and habits of play cannot be

trusted to develop habits of work. Our
efforts to protect the child from doing
what he does not want to do, because he
does not want to do it, are kind, but un-
intelligent. Life is not a vapid thing.
"The world," says Emerson, "is a proud
place, peopled with men of positive quality." No pleasure it can give, from the
time we are seven until the time we are
seventy, is comparable to the pleasure
of achievement.

Dr. Münsterberg, observing with dis-
may the "pedagogical unrest" which
pervades our communities, expresses a
naïve surprise that so much sound advice,
and so much sound instruction, should
leave the teacher without inspiration or
enthusiasm. "The pile of interesting facts
which the sciences heap up for the teacher's use grows larger and larger, but the
teacher seems to stare at it with growing
hopelessness."

I should think so. A pile of heterogeneous facts — segments of segments

Popular Education

of subjects — reduces any sane teacher to hopelessness, because he, at least, is well aware that his pupils cannot possibly absorb or digest a tithe of the material pressed upon their acceptance. Experience has taught him something which his counsellors never learn, — the need of limit, the "feasibility of performance." Hear what one teacher, both sane and experienced, has to say concerning the riot of facts and theories, of art and nature, of science and sentiment, which the school is expected to reduce into an orderly, consistent, and practical system of education.

"It is not enough that the child should be taught to handle skilfully the tools of all learning, — reading, writing, and arithmetic. His sense of form and his æsthetic nature must be developed by drawing; his hand must be trained by manual work; his musical nature must be awakened by song; he must be brought into harmony with his external environment by means of nature lessons and the study of science; his patriotic impulses must be roused by American history and by flag-drills; temperance must be instilled into him by lessons in physiology, with special reference to the effects of alcohol on the human system; his imagination must be cultivated by the help of Greek and Norse mythology; he must gain some knowledge of the great heroes and events of general history; he must acquire a love for and an appreciation of the best literature through the plentiful reading of masterpieces, while at the same time his mind should be stocked with choice gems of prose and verse, which will be a solace to him throughout his later life.

"It might be well if, by displacing a little arithmetic or geography, he could gain some knowledge of the elements of Latin or of a modern language; in some manner there must be roused in him a love for trees, a respect for birds, an an-

Popular Education

tipathy to cigarettes, and an ambition for clean streets; and somewhere, somewhere in this mad chaos he must learn to spell! Do you wonder that teachers in progressive schools confide to us that they fear their pupils are slightly bewildered? Do you wonder that pupils do not gain the habit and the power of concentrated, consecutive work?"[1]

And this irrational, irrelevant medley, this educational vaudeville, must be absorbed unconsciously, and without effort, by children roused to interest by the sustained enthusiasm of their teachers, whom may Heaven help! If the programme is not full enough, it can be varied by lectures on sex-hygiene, lessons in woodcraft (with reference to boy scouts), and pictures illustrating the domestic habits of the house-fly. These, with plenty of gymnastics, and a little barefoot dancing for girls, may bring a

[1] *The Existing Relations beween School and College,* by Wilson Farrand.

Counter-Currents

school measurably near the ideal proposed by Judge Lindsey,—a place where "there is something moving, something doing all the time," and which finds its closest counterpart in the rushing of engines on their tracks.

The theory that school work must appeal to a child's fluctuating tastes, must attract a child's involuntary attention, does grievous wrong to the rising generation; yet it is upheld in high places, and forms the subject-matter of many addresses vouchsafed year after year to long-suffering educators. They should bring to bear the "energizing force of interest," they should magnetize their pupils into work. Even Dr. Eliot reminds them with just a hint of reproach that, if a child is interested, he will not be disorderly; and this reiterated statement appears to be the crux of the whole difficult situation. Let us boldly suppose that a child is not interested, — and he may conceivably weary even of films, —

Popular Education

is it then optional with him to be, or not to be, disorderly, and what is the effect of his disorder on other children whose tastes may differ from his own?

The Right Reverend Mandell Creighton, who appears to have made more addresses to the teachers of England than any other ecclesiastic of his day, repeatedly warned them that they should not attempt to teach any subject without first making clear to children why this subject should command attention. If they failed to do so, said the bishop triumphantly, the children would not attend. He was of the opinion that little pupils must not only be rationally convinced that what they are asked to do is worth their doing, but that they must enjoy every step of their progress. A teacher who could not make a child feel that it is "just as agreeable" to be in school as at play, had not begun his, or her, pedagogical career.

This is a hard saying and a false one. Every normal child prefers play to work, and the precise value of work lies in its call for renunciation. Nor has any knowledge ever been acquired and retained without endeavour. What heroic pains were taken by Montaigne's father to spare his little son the harsh tasks of the school-boy! At what trouble and cost to the household was the child taught "the pure Latin tongue" in infancy, "without bookes, rules, or grammar, without whipping or whining"! Greek was also imparted to him in kindly fashion, "by way of sporte and recreation." "We did tosse our declinations and conjugations to and fro, as they doe, who, by means of a certaine game at tables, learne both Arithmeticke and Geometrie." Assuredly the elder Montaigne was a man born out of date. In our happier age he would have been a great and honoured upholder of educational novelties, experimenting with the school-rooms of the world. In the sixteenth century he was only a country gentleman, experimenting with his son,—

a son who bluntly confesses that, of the Greek thus pleasantly trifled with, he had "but small understanding," and that the Latin which had been his mother tongue was speedily "corrupted by discontinuance."

All the boy gained by the most elaborate system ever devised for the saving of labour was that he "overskipped" the lower forms in school. What he lost was the habit of mastering his "prescript lessons," which he seems to have disliked as heartily as any student of Guienne. Neither loss nor gain mattered much to a man of original parts. The principal result of his father's scheme was the lingering of certain Latin words among the simple folk of Perigord, who, having painfully acquired these strange terms in order to rescue their little master from his schoolbooks, retained and made use of them all their lives.

An emphatic note of protest against our well-meant but enfeebling educa-

Counter-Currents

tional methods was struck by Professor William James in his "Talks to Teachers," published in 1899. The phrase "Economy of Effort," so dear to the kindly hearts of Froebel's followers, had no meaning for Dr. James. The ingenious system by which the child's tasks, as well as the child's responsibilities, are shifted to the shoulders of the teacher, made no appeal to his incisive intelligence. He stoutly asserted that effort is oxygen to the lungs of youth, and that it is sheer nonsense to suppose that every step of education can possibly be made interesting. The child, like the man, must meet his difficulties, and master them. There is no lesson worth learning, no game worth playing, which does not call for exertion. Rousseau, it will be remembered, would not permit Émile to know what rivalry meant. That harassed child never even ran a race, lest the base spirit of competition should penetrate his nerveless little being. But Professor James, deaf

Popular Education

to social sentimentalities, averred that rivalry is the spur of action, and the impelling force of civilization. "There is a noble and generous kind of rivalry as well as a spiteful and greedy kind," he wrote truthfully, "and the noble and generous form is particularly common in childhood. All games owe the zest which they bring with them to the fact that they are rooted in the emulous passion, yet they are the chief means of training in fairness and magnanimity."

I am aware that it is a dangerous thing to call kindness sentimental; but our feeling that children have a right to happiness, and our sincere effort to protect them from any approach to pain, have led imperceptibly to the elimination from their lives of many strength-giving influences. A recent volume on "Child Culture" (a phrase every whit as reprehensible as "child-material") speaks always of naughty children as "patients," implying that their unfortunate condition

Counter-Currents

is involuntary, and must be cured from
without, not from within. The "rights of
children" include the doubtful privilege
of freedom from restraint, and the doubtful boon of shelter from obligation. It
seems sweet and kind to teach a child
high principles and steadfastness of purpose by means of symbolic games rather
than by any open exaction. Unconscious
obedience, like indirect taxation, is supposed to be paid without strain. Our
feverish fear lest we offend against the
helplessness of childhood, our feverish
concern lest it should be denied its full
measure of content, drive us, burdened
as we are with good intentions, past the
border-line of wisdom. If we were

"Less winning soft, less amiably mild,"

we might see more clearly the value of
standards.

Two years ago I had sent me several
numbers of a Los Angeles newspaper.
They contained a spirited and sympa-

Popular Education

thetic account of a woman who had been arrested for stealing a child's outfit, and who pleaded in court that she wanted the garments for her daughter, the little girl having refused to go to school, because other children had laughed at her shabby clothes. The effect of this pathetic disclosure was instantaneous and overwhelming. The woman was released, and kind-hearted people hastened to send "nicey" frocks by the "wagon-load" to the ill-used child. A picture of the heroic mother in a large plumed hat, and another of little Ellen in curls and hair-ribbons, occupied prominent places in the paper. The public mind was set at rest concerning the quality of the goods donated. "Ellen is going to school to-day," wrote the jubilant reporter. "She is going to wear a fluffy new dress with lace, and hair-ribbons to match. And if any rude boy so far forgets himself as to tear that wondrous creation, there will be others at home to replace it. Happy, oh,

Counter-Currents

so happy was the little miss, as she shook her curls over the dainty dress to-day. And the mother? Well, a faith in the inherent goodness of mankind has been rekindled in her bosom."

Now the interesting thing about this journalistic eloquence, and the public sentiment it represented, is that while shabbiness was admittedly a burden too heavy for a child to bear, theft carried with it no shadow of disgrace. Children might jeer at a little girl in a worn frock, but a little girl in "lace and hair-ribbons" was manifestly above reproach. Her mother's transgression had covered her with glory, not with shame. There seems to be some confusion of standards in such a verdict, some deviation from the paths of rectitude and honour. It is hard for a child to be more poorly dressed than her companions; but to convince her that dishonesty is the best policy and brings its own reward, is but a dubious kindness. Nor is it impossible

Popular Education

to so stiffen her moral fibre that her poor dress may be worn, if not with pride, at least with sturdy self-control.

On this point I know whereof I speak, for, when I was a little girl, my convent school sheltered a number of Southern children, reduced to poverty by the Civil War, and educated (though of this no one was aware) by the boundless charity of the nuns. These children were shabby, with a pathetic shabbiness which fell far below our very moderate requirements. Their dresses (in my prehistoric days, school uniforms were worn only on Thursdays and Sundays) were strangely antiquated, as though cut down from the garments of mothers and grandmothers, their shoes were scuffed, their hats were hopeless. But the unquenchable pride with which they bore themselves invested such hardships with distinction. Their poverty was the honourable outcome of war; and this fact, added to their simple and sincere conviction that a girl born below the Mason and Dixon line must necessarily be better than a girl born above it, carried them unscathed through the valley of humiliation. Looking back now with an unbiassed mind, I am disposed to consider their claim to superiority unfounded; but, at the time, their single - mindedness carried conviction. The standards they imposed were preeminently false, but they were less ignoble than the standards imposed by wealth. No little American boy or girl can know to-day what it means to have the character set in childhood by history, by the vividness of early years lived under strange and violent conditions, by the sufferings, the triumphs, the high and sad emotions of war.

There is a story told by Sir Francis Doyle which illustrates, after the rude fashion of our forebears, the value of endurance as an element of education. Dr. Keate, the terrible head-master of Eton, encountered one winter morning a small

Popular Education

boy crying miserably, and asked him
what was the matter. The child replied
that he was cold. "Cold!" roared Keate.
"You must put up with cold, sir! You
are not at a girls' school."

It is a horrid anecdote, and I am kind-
hearted enough to wish that Dr. Keate,
who was not without his genial moods,
had taken the lad to some generous fire
(presuming such a thing was to be found),
and had warmed his frozen hands and
feet. But it so chanced that in that little
snivelling boy there lurked a spark of
pride and a spark of fun, and both ignited
at the rough touch of the master. He
probably stopped crying, and he certainly
remembered the sharp appeal to manhood. Fifteen years later he charged
with the Third Dragoons at the strongly
entrenched Sikhs (thirty thousand of the
best fighting men of the Khalsa) on the
curving banks of the Sutlej. When
the word was given, he turned to his
superior officer, a fellow Etonian who

was scanning the stout walls and the belching guns. "As old Keate would say, this is no girls' school," he chuckled ; and rode to his death on the battlefield of Sobraon, which gave Lahore to England.

Contemplating which incident, and many like it, we become aware that ease is not the only good in a world consecrated to the heroic business of living and of dying.

The Modest Immigrant

IT is now nearly fifty years since Mr. Lowell wrote his famous essay, "On a Certain Condescension in Foreigners"; an essay in which justifiable irritation prompted the telling of plain truths, and an irrepressible sense of humour made these truths amusing. It was well for Mr. Lowell that he was seldom too angry to laugh, and he knew, as only a man of the world can know, the saving grace of laughter. Therefore, though confessedly unable to understand why foreigners should be persuaded that "by doing this country the favour of coming to it, they have laid every native thereof under an obligation," he was willing in certain light-minded moods to acquit himself honourably of the debt. When a genteel German mendicant presented a letter, "professedly written by a benev-

Counter-Currents

olent American clergyman," and certifying that the bearer thereof had long "sofered with rheumatic paints in his limps," Mr. Lowell rightly considered that a composition so rich in the naïveté common to all Teuton mendacities was worth the money asked. When a French traveller assured him, with delightful *bonhomie*, that Englishmen became Americanized so rapidly that "they even begin to talk through their noses, just like you do," the only comment of our representative American was that he felt ravished by this testimony to the assimilating powers of democracy.

Nevertheless, it is well in these years of grace to reread Mr. Lowell's essay, partly because of its sturdy and dignified Americanism, and partly because we can then compare his limited experiences with our own. We can also speculate pleasantly upon his frame of mind could he have lived to hear Mrs. Amadeus Grabau (Mary Antin) say, "Lowell would

The Modest Immigrant

agree with me,"—the point of agreement being the relative virtues of the Pilgrim Fathers and the average immigrant of to-day. When the dead are quoted in this fashion and nothing happens, then we know that, despite the assurances of Sir Oliver Lodge, the seal of silence is unbroken. Were the proud souls who have left us, able and willing to return, it would not be to reveal the whereabouts of a lost penknife, but to give the lie to the words which are spoken in their name.

The condescension which Mr. Lowell observed and analyzed was in his day the shining quality of foreigners who visit our shores. Immigrants were then less aggressive and less profoundly self-conscious than they are now, and it is the immigrant who counts. It is his arrogance, not the misapprehension of the tourist, or the innocent pride of the lecturer, which constitutes a peril to our republic. We can all of us afford to smile

Counter-Currents

with Mr. Lowell at the men and women
who, while accepting our hospitality,
"make no secret of regarding us as the
goose bound to deliver them a golden
egg in return for their cackle." That they
should not hesitate to come without
equipment, without experience, without
even a fitness for their task, seems to us
perfectly natural. Perhaps they have written books which none of us have read, or
edited periodicals which none of us have
seen. Perhaps they have known celeb-
rities of whom few of us have heard. It
does not matter in the least. From the
days when Miss Rose Kingsley came to
tell us the worth of French art (does not
the ocean roll between New York and
Paris?), to the days when Mrs. Pankhurst
came to tell us the worth of womanhood
(does not the ocean roll between Boston
Common and Hyde Park?), we have listened patiently, and paid generously, and
received scant courtesy for our pains. "I
find it so strange," said an Englishman

The Modest Immigrant

to me three years ago, "to see my wife lecturing over the United States. It is a thing she would not dream of doing at home. In fact, nobody would go to hear her, you know."

But lectures are transient things, forgiven as soon as forgotten. Even the books which are written about us make no painful bid for immortality. And though our visitors patronize us, they seldom fail to throw us a kind word now and then. Sometimes a sweet-tempered and very hurried traveller, like Mr. Arnold Bennett, is good enough to praise everything he thinks he has seen. Before August, 1914, it was not the habit of our guests to scold or threaten us. That privilege had hitherto been reserved for the alien, who, having done us the honour of accepting citizenship, wields his vote as a cudgel, bidding us beware the weapon we have amiably placed in his hands.

Signor Ferrero, an acute and friendly critic, pronounces Americans to be the

Counter-Currents

mystics of the modern world, because they sacrifice their welfare to a sentiment; because they believe in the miracle of the melting-pot, which, like Medea's magic cauldron, will turn the old and decrepit races of Europe into a young and vigorous people, new-born in soul and body. No other nation cherishes this illusion. An Englishman knows that a Russian Jew cannot in five years, or in twenty-five years, become English; that his standards and ideals are not convertible into English standards and ideals. A Frenchman does not see in a Bulgarian or a Czech the making of another Frenchman. Our immigrants may be as good as we are. Sometimes we are told they are better, that we might "learn a lesson" from the least promising among them. But no one can deny that they are different; in many instances, radically and permanently different. And to make a sow's ear out of a silk purse is just as difficult as the reverse operation. Mr.

The Modest Immigrant

Horace Kallen has put the case into a few clear conclusive words when he says, "Only men who are alike in origin and spirit, and not abstractly, can be truly equal, and maintain that inward unanimity of action and outlook which makes a national life."

To look for "inward unanimity" among the seething mass of immigrants who have nothing more in common with one another than they have with us, is to tax credulity too far. The utmost we can hope is that their mutual antagonisms will neutralize their voting power, and keep our necks free from an alien yoke. Those of us who have lived more than half a century have seen strange fluctuations in the fortunes of the foreign-born. In 1883, when the Brooklyn Bridge was finished, the Irishmen of New York made a formal protest against its being opened on Queen Victoria's birthday, lest this chance occurrence should be misconstrued into a compliment to

Counter-Currents

England. In 1915, a band in Saint Patrick's parade was halted, and forbidden to play " Tipperary " before Cardinal Farley's residence, lest these cheerful strains should be misconstrued into an insult to Germany. The Reverend Thomas Thornton, speaking to the Knights of Columbus, prophesied mournfully that the time was at hand when Catholic voters in the United States would be " reduced to the condition of tribute-paying aliens." Men smiled when they heard this, reflecting that the Irish officeholder had not yet been consigned to oblivion ; but the speaker had seen with a clear eye the marshalling of strange forces, destined to drive the first comer from authority. Some weeks later, the " Jewish Tribune " boasted that the angry protest voiced by Catholics against the sending of Signor Ernesto Nathan as commissioner to the San Francisco Fair had been " checked in its infancy " by the power of the Jewish press.

The Modest Immigrant

It is all very lively and interesting, but where does the American come in? What place is reserved for him in the commonwealth which his heroic toil and heroic sacrifices moulded into what Washington proudly called a "respectable nation"? The truth is contemptuously flung at us by Mary Antin, when she says that the descendants of the men who made America are not numerous enough to "swing a presidential election." And if a negligible factor now, what depths of insignificance will be their portion in the future? I heard told with glee — the glee which expresses pure American unconcern — a story of a public school in one of our large eastern cities. A visitor of an investigating turn of mind asked the pupils of various nationalities, Germans, Polacks, Russian Jews, Italians, Armenians and Greeks, to stand up in turn. When the long list was seemingly exhausted, he bethought himself of a nation he had overlooked, and said, "Now

let the American children arise !" Whereupon one lone, lorn little black boy stood
up to represent the native-born.

It is hardly surprising that these foreign children, recognizing the strength
of numbers, should take exception to
our time-honoured methods of education. Little boys of a socialistic turn of
mind refuse to salute the flag, because it
is a military emblem. Little boys of a
rationalistic turn of mind refuse to read
the Bible, — any portion of the Bible, —
because its assertions are unscientific.
Little Jewish boys and girls refuse to
sing the " Battle Hymn of the Republic,"
because of its unguarded allusions to
Bethlehem and Calvary. Indeed, any
official recognition of the Deity offends
the susceptibilities of some of our future
citizens ; and their perplexed teachers
are bidden to eliminate from their programme "any exercises which the pupils
consider objectionable."

A few years ago I was asked to speak

The Modest Immigrant

to a large class of immigrant working-girls, for whose benefit philanthropic women had planned evening classes, dexterously enlivened by a variety of entertainments. I was not sure whether I ranked as useful or amusing, and the number of topics I was bidden to tactfully avoid, added to my misgivings; when suddenly all doubts were dispelled by the superintendent saying sweetly, "Oh, Miss Repplier, you were asked to speak for forty minutes; but I think your address had better be cut down to twenty-five. The girls are eager for their ice-cream."

I said I sympathized with so reasonable an impatience. Even at my advanced age, I prefer ice-cream to lectures.

> "Moi, je dis que les bonbons
> Valent mieux que la raison."

But what did not flatter me was the clear understanding that my audience listened to me, or at least sat tolerantly for twenty

Counter-Currents

minutes (I curtailed my already cur-tail'd cur), because their reward, in the shape of ice-cream, was near at hand. Just as some manufacturers provide baths for their employees, and then, recognizing the prejudices of the foreign-born, pay the men for taking the baths provided, so the good ladies who had served me up as a mental refreshment for their protégées, paid the girls for being so obliging as to listen to me.

Miss Addams has reproached us most unjustly for our contemptuous disregard of the immigrant; and Mrs. Percy Pennybacker, president of the General Federation of Women's Clubs, has been wrought to such a pitch of indignation over what she considers our unwarranted superciliousness, that she writes fervidly in the "Ladies' Home Journal," "I love my country; I adore her; but at times I hope that some great shock may cause us to drop the mantle of conceit that we so proudly wrap about us."

The Modest Immigrant

This well-wisher is in a fair way to see her desires realized. We may be left naked and shivering sooner than she anticipates. If concessions to the Irish vote failed to teach us humility, — perhaps because the Irish have a winning way of overriding barriers ("What's the Constitution between friends?"), — other immigrants are less urbane in stripping us of our pride. "A German," said Mr. Lowell feelingly, "is not always nice in concealing his contempt"; and if this was his attitude in 1868, to what superb heights of disdain has he risen by 1916! A German ambassador has derided diplomatic conventions, and has addressed his official communication, over the head of the Administration, to German voters in the United States, sparing no pains to make his words offensive. German officials have sought to undermine our neutrality and imperil our safety. In the opening months of the war, a German professor at Harvard, who for years has

Counter-Currents

received courteous and honourable treatment at the hands of Americans, threatened us insolently with the "crushing power" of the German vote; and bade us beware of the punishment which twenty-five millions of citizens, "in whose homes lives the memory of German ancestors," would inflict upon their fellow citizens of less august and martial stock. The "Frankfurter Zeitung" published a cheering letter from an American Congressman, assuring a German correspondent that his countrymen know how to make themselves heard, and expressing hearty hopes that Germany would triumph over her "perfidious" rival.

Is it any wonder that, stimulated by these brilliant examples, the average "German-American" should wax scornful, and despise his unhyphenated fellow citizens? Is it any wonder that he should turn bully, and threaten us with his vote, — the vote which was confided to his sacred honour for the preservation of our

The Modest Immigrant

country's liberty? A circular distributed
before the Chicago elections in 1915
stated in the plainest possible words that
the German's first allegiance was to imperial Germany, and not to the Republic
he had sworn to serve : —

"Chicago has a larger German population than any city in the world, except-
ing Berlin and Vienna ; and the German-,
Austrian-, and Hungarian - Americans
should, at this coming election, *set aside
every other consideration*, and vote as a
unit for Robert M. Sweitzer. Stand
shoulder to shoulder in this election, as
our countrymen in the trenches and on
the high seas are fighting for the preservation of our dear Fatherland. The
election of a German-American would
be a fitting answer to the defamers of
the Fatherland, would cause a tremen-
dous moral effect throughout the United
States, and would reëcho in Germany,
Austria, and Hungary."

The " moral effect " of this appeal was

not precisely what its authors had antici-
pated. Men asked themselves in bewil-
derment and wrath what the dear Fatherland, any more than dear Dahomey or
the beloved Congo, had to do with the
Chicago elections? They have been putting similar questions ever since.

Some months later, the German-American Central Society of Passaic, uniting
itself with the German-American National Alliance, called for assistance in
these glowing words: —

"Come all of you German societies,
German men, and German women, so
that united offensively and defensively
[*zum Schutz und Trutz verein*] with
weapons of the spirit, we may help our
beloved Germany onward."

"Weapons of the spirit!" If this means
prayer and supplication, the matter lies
between the petitioner and his God. If
it means exhortations, pamphlets, and
platform oratory, the champion of Germany stands well within his rights. But

The Modest Immigrant

the next paragraph drops all figures of speech, and states the real issue with abrupt and startling distinctness : —

" We ask for your speedy decision with respect to your acquiescence, in order to permit of an effective participation and lead in the spring campaign of 1915."

In plain words, the spiritual weapon with which the German-American proposes to fight the battle of Germany is the American ballot. When the franchise was granted to him, or to his father, or to his grandfather (whichever did this country the honour of first accepting citizenship), a solemn oath was sworn. Allegiance to a foreign government was forever disowned ; fealty to the government of the United States was vowed. He who uses his vote to further the interests of a European state is a perjured man, and that he should dare to threaten us with the power of his perjury is the height of arrogant ill-doing. That such a question as " What is the proportion of

Counter-Currents

votes which the Germans of your section control?" should be asked by German agents, and answered by German newspapers, affronts our nation's honour, soils a sacred trust by ill-usage, and tears our neutrality to rags.

When the Lusitania was sunk, and the horror of the deed shamed all Christendom, save only those strange residents of Berlin who received the news with "enthusiasm," and "joyful pride," the first word tactfully whispered in our ear was that, while we might regret the drowning of Americans, we were impotent to resent it. And this impotence was to be a concession to the foreign vote. God only knows of what material Germany thought we were made, — putty, or gutta-percha, or sun-baked mud? Certainly not of flesh and blood. Certainly not with hearts to bleed, or souls to burn. Every comment vouchsafed by the German press placed us in the catalogue of worms warranted not to turn.

The Modest Immigrant

The contempt which the German "is not always nice in concealing" shines with a chastened lustre in the words and deeds of other foreign - born citizens. They accept the vote which we enthusiastically press upon them, regarding it as an asset, sometimes of marketable value, sometimes serving a stronger and more enduring purpose, always as an esteemed protection against the military service exacted by their own governments. They do not come to us "with gifts in their hands," — to quote Mr. Lowell. They are for the most part destitute, not only of money, but of knowledge, of useful attainments, of any serviceable mental equipment. Mr. Edward Alsworth Ross, who is not without experience, confesses ruefully that the immigrant seldom brings in his intellectual baggage anything of use to us; and that the admission into our electorate of "backward men" — men whose mental, moral, and physical standards are lower than our own — must inevitably retard our social progress, and thrust us behind the more uniformly civilized nations of the world.

Meditating on these disagreeable facts, we find ourselves confronted by sentimentalists who say that if we would only be kind and brotherly, the sloping foreheads would grow high, the narrow shoulders broad, the Pole would become peaceable, the Greek honest, the Slav clean, the Sicilian would give up murder as a pastime, the Jew would lose his "monstrous love of gain." Enthusiastic promoters of the "National Americanization Committee" — a crusade full of promise for the future — have talked to us so much and so sternly about our duty to the immigrant, our neglect of the immigrant, our debt to the immigrant, our need of the immigrant, that we have been no less humiliated than bewildered by their eloquence. Mr. Roosevelt alone, of all their orators, has had the hardihood to say bluntly that citizenship implies

The Modest Immigrant

service as well as protection; that the debt contracted by the citizen to the state is as binding as that contracted by the state to the citizen; that a voter who cannot speak English is an absurdity no less than a peril; and that all who seek the franchise should be compelled to accept without demur our laws, our language, our national policy, our requisitions civil and military. This is what naturalization implies.

That saving phrase, "It is the law," which made possible the civilization of Rome, and which has been the foundation of all great civilizations before and since, has little weight or sanctity for our immigrants. They resent legal interference, especially the punishment of crime, in a very spirited fashion. When Mr. Samuel Gompers defended the McNamaras and their "social war" murders before a subcommittee of the United States Senate, he said with feeling that the mere fact that these men should have

217

Counter-Currents

come to look upon dynamite as the only defence left them against the tyranny of capital, was a "terrible charge against society." It was an appeal very pleasantly suggestive of the highwayman, who, having attacked and robbed Lord Derby and Mr. Grenville, said reproachfully to his victims, "What scoundrels you must be to fire at a gentleman who risks his life upon the road!"

If Cicero lowered his voice when he spoke of the Jews, fearing the enmity of this strong and clannish people, the American, who is far from enjoying Cicero's prestige, must be doubly cautious lest he give offence. Yet surely, if there is an immigrant who owes us everything, it is the Jew. Even our spasmodic and utterly futile efforts to restrict immigration always leave him a loophole of escape, because he controls the National Liberal Immigration League.

It is our custom to assume that the Russian Jew is invariably a fugitive from

The Modest Immigrant

religious persecution, and we liken him in this regard to the best and noblest of our early settlers. But the Puritan, the Quaker, and the Huguenot sacrificed temporal well-being for liberty of conscience. They left conditions of comfort, and the benefits of a high civilization, to develop the resources of a virgin land, and build for themselves homes in the wilderness. They practised the stern virtues of courage, fortitude, and a most splendid industry. Had the Pilgrim Fathers been met on Plymouth Rock by immigration officials; had their children been placed immediately in good free schools, and given the care of doctors, dentists, and nurses; had they found themselves in infinitely better circumstances than they had ever enjoyed in England, indulging in undreamed-of luxuries, and taught by kind-hearted philanthropists, — what pioneer virtues would they have developed, what sons would they have bred, what honours would history have accorded them? If our early settlers were masterful, they earned the right to mastery, and the price they paid for it was endurance. To the sacrifices which they made, to their high courage and heroic labours, we owe law, liberty, and well-being.

It is because the Jew has received from us so much, and given us so little, that his masterfulness affronts our sense of decency. When the Jewish Anti-Defamation League boasts — perhaps without warranty — that it has taken "the first and most important step in excluding the 'Merchant of Venice' from the curriculum of the grammar and high schools of this country, by having the play removed from the list of requirements laid down by the Collegiate Entrance Requirement Board," we feel that a joke has been carried too far. Nobody can seriously associate the " Merchant of Venice" with a defamation of the Jewish character. Heaven knows, the part

The Modest Immigrant

played by Christians in that immortal drama has never left us puffed up with pride. Nevertheless, being less thin-skinned, or perhaps more sure of ourselves, we have grown attached to the play, and should not relish its banishment by the decree of aliens.

And what if our Italian immigrants should take exception to the character of Iago, and demand that "Othello" should be excluded from the schools? What if the Sicilians should find themselves wounded in spirit by the behaviour of Leontes (compared with whom Shylock and Iago are gentlemen), and deny us the "Winter's Tale"? What if the Bohemians (a fast-increasing body of voters) should complain that their peddlers are honest men, shamefully slandered by the rogueries of Autolycus? If all our foreign citizens become in turn as sensitive as Hebrews, we may find ourselves reduced to the fairy scenes from the "Tempest" and the "Midsummer Night's Dream."

Counter-Currents

Another victory claimed by the "Jewish Tribune" is that the Associated Press has been made to feel that the words "Jew" and "Hebrew" should be avoided in connection with criminals. "The religious denomination of malefactors should not be referred to. It is now generally understood by newspapers that it is just as improper to describe a malefactor by stating that he is a Jew, as it would be to describe such a person as a Catholic or a Methodist."

Does this mean that the Jew no longer claims any racial distinction, that he has no genealogy, no pedigree, no place in history, nothing by which he may be classified but church membership? Is the simple dictionary definition, "Jew. An Israelite; a person of the Hebrew race," without any significance? We may call a Greek pickpocket a Greek, or a Polish rioter a Pole, or an Italian murderer an Italian; but we may not call a Jewish procurer a Jew, because that word re-

The Modest Immigrant

fers only to his attendance at the synagogue. May we then speak of a scholar, a musician, a scientist, a philanthropist, as a Jew? Only — by this ruling — as we might speak of one as a Catholic or a Methodist, only in reference to his "religious denomination." If he chances to be unsectarian, then, as he is also raceless, he cannot be called anything at all. If the word "Jew" be out of place in the police courts, it is equally out of place in colleges, learned societies, and encyclopædias.

It will be remembered that, after the publication of "Oliver Twist," a bitter protest was raised by English Jews against the character of Fagin, or rather against the fact that the merry old gentleman is alluded to frequently as a Jew. The complainants said — what the "Jewish Tribune" now says — that the use of the word as an indicatory substantive was an insult to their creed. Dickens, who had never thought of Fagin as having any creed, who had never associated him with religious observances of any kind, was puzzled and pained at having unwittingly given offence; and strove to make clear that, when he said "Jew," he meant an Israelite, and not a frequenter of the synagogue. Years afterward he made a peace-offering in the person of Riah, who plays the part of a good Samaritan in "Our Mutual Friend," and who is to Fagin as skimmed milk to brandy.

It is worthy of note that whenever any strong and noble emotion grips our Jewish citizens, they speedily forget their antipathy to the word "Jew." For years past they have objected to the use of the word by charitable associations, even when there was no hint of criminality to shame it. They have asked that visiting nurses should not report service to Jewish homes, or Jewish patients. Homes and patients should be placed upon record as Russian or Polish, — whichever the case might be. The race was specifically denied. The Semite was sunk in the

The Modest Immigrant

Slav. But when there came a cry for help from the war-stricken Jews of Europe, the Jews of America responded with exalted enthusiasm. Jew called to Jew, and the great tie of kindred asserted itself supremely. It was not as co-religionists, but as brothers-in-blood, that New York millionaires, who had never entered a synagogue, stretched out their hands in aid. Women stripped off their jewels, and offered this glittering tribute, as they might have done in the fighting days of Israel. Young and old, rich and poor, gave with unstinted compassion. Gentiles contributed generously to the fund, and Christian churches asked the coöperation of Christian congregations. To some Jews the thought must have occurred that America had not dealt harshly by her immigrants, when they could command millions for their impoverished brethren in Europe.

Therefore it behooves the men and women who have been well received, and

Counter-Currents

who have responded ably to the opportunities offered them by our country's superb liberality, to be a little more lenient to our shortcomings. We confess them readily enough; but we feel that those whom we have befriended should not be the ones to dwell upon them with too much gusto. There are situations in the world which imperiously dictate urbanity. "Steadily as I worked to win America," writes Mary Antin, "America advanced to lie at my feet," — a poodle-like attitude which ought to disarm criticism. When this clever young woman tells us that she "took possession of Beacon Street" (a goodly heritage), and there "drank afternoon tea with gentle ladies whose hands were as delicate as their porcelain cups," we feel well content at this swift recognition of energy and ability. It is not the first time such pleasant things have happened, and it will not be the last. But why should the recipient of so much attention be the one

The Modest Immigrant

to scold us harshly, to rail at conditions she imperfectly understands, to reproach us for our ill-mannered children (whom we fear she must have met in Beacon Street), our slackness in duty, our failure to observe the precepts and fulfil the intentions of those pioneers whom she kindly, but confusedly, calls "*our* forefathers."

It is the hopeless old story of opposing races, of people unable to understand one another because they have no mutual standards, no common denominator. Mary Antin is perfectly sincere, and, from her point of view, justified, in bidding us remember that among the Harrison Avenue tenants, "who pitch rubbish through their windows," was the grocer whose kindness helped to keep her at school. And she adds with sublime because unconscious egotism, "Let the City Fathers strike the balance." But Elizabeth Robins Pennell is also sincere, and, from *her* point of view, justified, when she says with exceeding bitterness that,

Counter-Currents

if Philadelphia blossomed like the rose
with Mary Antins, the city would be but
ill repaid for the degradation of her noble
old streets, now transformed into foul and
filthy slums. Dirt is a valuable asset in
the immigrant's hands. With its help
he drives away decent neighbours, and
brings property down to his level and
his purse. The ill-fated Philadelphian is
literally pushed out of his home — the
only place, sighs Mrs. Pennell, where he
wants to live — by conditions which he
is unable to avert, and unwilling, as well
as unfitted, to endure.

It is part of the unreality of modern
sentimentalism that we should have a
strong sense of duty toward all the nations of the world except our own. We
see plainly what we owe to the Magyar
and the Levantine, but we have no concern for the Virginian or the Pennsyl-
vanian. The capitalist and the sentimentalist play into each other's hands, and
neither takes thought of our country's

The Modest Immigrant

irrational present and imperilled future. We go on keeping a "civic kindergarten" for backward aliens, and we go on mutely suffering reproach for not advancing our pupils more rapidly. In the industrial town of New Britain, Connecticut, the foreign population is nine times greater than the native population, which is a hideous thing to contemplate. Twenty nationalities are represented, eighteen languages are spoken. The handful of Americans, who are supposed to leaven this heavy and heterogeneous mass, take their duties very seriously. Schools, playgrounds, clubs, night-classes, vacation classes, gymnasiums, visiting nurses, milk-stations, charitable organizations, a city mission with numerous interpreters, a free library with books and newspapers in divers tongues, all the leavening machinery is kept in active service for the hard task of civic betterment. Yet it was in New Britain that an immigrant was found who, after sixteen years' residence

Counter-Currents

in the United States, was not aware that he might, if he chose, become a citizen; and this incident, Mary Antin considers a heavy indictment against the community. "It makes a sensitive American," she writes passionately, "choke with indignation."

It makes an exasperated American choke with angry laughter to have the case put that way. The ballot is not necessary to safe, decent, and prosperous living. A good many millions of women have made shift to live safely, decently, and prosperously without it. If it is to be regarded as an asset to the immigrant, then his own friends, his own people, the voters of his own race, might (in the welcome absence of political bosses) be the ones to press it upon his acceptance. If it be considered as a safeguard for the Republic, we cannot but feel that this highly intelligent alien might be spared permanently from the electorate.

For the first nine months of the war,

The Modest Immigrant

when Italy's neutrality swayed in the conflicting currents of national pride and national precaution, and no one could foretell what the end would be, a young Italian gardener, employed near Philadelphia, suffered dismal doubts concerning the expediency of naturalization. He was a frugal person, devoid of high political instincts. He did not covet a vote to sell, and he did not want to pay the modest cost of becoming an American citizen. He preferred keeping his money and staying what he was, provided always that Italy remained at peace. But the prospect of Italy's going to war disposed him to look favourably upon the safeguard of a foreign allegiance. Being unable to decipher the newspapers, he made anxious inquiries every morning. If the headlines read, "Italy unlikely to abandon attitude of neutrality," he settled down contentedly to his day's work. If the headlines read, "Austria refuses guarantee. Italy sending troops to northern frontier," he became once more a prey to indecision. Then came the May days when doubt was turned to certainty. Italy, long straining at the leash, plunged into the conflict. Thousands of Italians in the United States stood ready to fight for their country, to give back to her, if need be, the lives which they might have held safe. But one peace-loving gardener hurried to Philadelphia, applied for his naturalization papers, failed utterly to pass the casual tests which would have secured them, grew frightened and demoralized by failure, appealed desperately to his employer, and, with a little timely aid, was pitched shivering into citizenship.

If ever there comes a cloud between the United States and Italy, this doughty "Italian-American" will, I am sure, be found fighting with "weapons of the spirit" for the welfare of his adored and endangered "Fatherland."

Waiting

I N the most esteemed of his advisory poems, Mr. Longfellow recommends his readers to be "up and doing," and at the same time learn "to labour and to wait." Having, all of us, imbibed these sentiments in their harmonious setting when we were at school, we have, all of us, endeavoured for many months to put such conflicting precepts into practice. Mr. Longfellow, it will be remembered, gave precedence to his "up and doing" line; but this may have been due to the exigencies of verse. We began by waiting, and we waited long. Our deliberation has seemed to border on paralysis. But back of this superhuman patience — rewarded by repeated insult and repeated injury — was a toughening resolution which snatched from insult and injury the bitter fruit of knowledge. We are emerging from this period of suspense a sadder and a wiser people, keenly aware of dangers which, a year ago, seemed negligible, fully determined to front such dangers with courage and with understanding.

When Germany struck her first blow at Belgium, the neutral nations silently acquiesced in this breach of good faith. The burning of Louvain, the destruction of the Cathedral of Rheims, were but the first fruits of this sinister silence. The sinking of the Lusitania followed in the orderly sequence of events. It was a deliberate expression of defiance and contempt, a gauntlet thrown to the world. The lives it cost, the innocence and helplessness of the drowned passengers, their number and their nationalities, all combined to make this novelty in warfare exactly what Germany meant it to be. We Americans had tried (and it had been hard work) to bear tranquilly the misfortunes of others. Now let us apply our philos-

Waiting

ophy to ourselves. Herr Erich von Salz-
mann voiced the sentiment of his countrymen when he said in the Berlin " Lokal
Anzeiger " : —

"The Lusitania is no more. Only those
who have travelled by sea can appreciate
the extraordinary impression which this
news will make all over the world. . . .
The fact that it was we Germans who
destroyed this ship must make us proud
of ourselves. The Lusitania case will ob-
tain for us more respect than a hundred
battles won on land."

The severing of fear from respect is a
subtlety which has not penetrated the
mind of the Prussian. He recognizes no
such distinction, because his doctrine of
efficiency embraces the doctrine of frightfulness. His Kultur is free from any
ethical bias. The fact that we may greatly
fear lust, cruelty, and other forms of violence, without in the least respecting these
qualities, has no significance for him.
He frankly does not care. If he can teach

Counter-Currents

the French, the English, or the Americans to fear him in 1916, as he taught the Chinese to fear him in 1900, and by the same methods, he will be well content.

But was it fear which paralyzed us when we heard that American women and children had been sacrificed as ruthlessly as were the Chinese women and children sixteen years ago? The fashion in which American gentlemen died on the Lusitania, as on the Titanic, may well acquit us of any charge of cowardice. Whatever "respect" ensued from that pitiless massacre was won by the victims, not by the perpetrators thereof. Why, then, when the news was brought, did we feverishly urge one another to "keep calm"? Why did we chatter day after day about "rocking the boat," as though unaware that the blow which sent us reeling and quivering was struck by a foreign hand? Why did we let pass the supreme moment of action, and settle down to

Waiting

months of controversy? And what have we gained by delay?

All these questions have been answered many times to the satisfaction and dissatisfaction of the querists. If we had severed diplomatic and commercial relations with Germany, she might have declared war, and we did not want to fight; not, at least, on such provocation as she had given us, and with such ships and munitions as we could command. There was a well-founded conviction that no step involving the safety of the nation should be taken impetuously, or under the influence of resentment, or without discreet calculation of ways and means. There was also a rational hope that Germany might be induced to disavow the savage slaughter of noncombatants, and promise redress. And always in the background of our consciousness was a lurking hope that the pen would prove mightier than the sword. The copybooks say that it is mightier, and where

Counter-Currents

shall we look for wisdom, if not to the counsels of the copy-book!

The correspondence which ensued between the Administration in Washington and the Imperial Government in Berlin was so remarkable that it may well serve as a model for generations yet unborn. If the Polite Letter-Writer ever broadens its sphere to embrace diplomatic relations, it could not do better than reprint these admirable specimens of what was thought to be a lost art. The urbanity and firmness of each American note filled us with justifiable pride. Also with a less justifiable elation, which was always dissipated by the arrival of a German note, equally urbane and equally firm. Germany was more than willing to state at length and at leisure her reasons for sinking merchant ships, provided she could safely and uninterruptedly continue the practice. Such warfare she defined in her note of July 9 as a "sacred duty." "If the Imperial

Waiting

Government were derelict in these duties, it would be guilty before God and history of the violation of those principles of highest humanity which are the foundation of every national existence."

The German is certainly at home in Zion. If his god be a trifle exacting in the matter of human sacrifice, he is otherwise the most pliant and accommodating of deities. It is one of our many disadvantages that we have no American god. Only the Divinity, whose awful name is, by comment consent, omitted from diplomatic correspondence.

When our hopes sank lowest and our hearts burned hottest, the note of September 1, 1915, brought its welcome message of concession. It is as little worth while to analyze the motives which prompted this change of front as it is worth while to speculate upon its sincerity. In the light of subsequent events, we are painfully aware that our satisfaction was excessive, our self-congratulations

Counter-Currents

unwarranted, our jubilant editorials a trifle overcharged. But at the time we believed what we wanted to believe, we joyfully assumed that Germany had been converted to the ways of humanity, and that she stood ready to anger her own people for the sake of conciliating ours.

Why the submarine warfare should have so endeared itself to the Teuton heart is a problem for psychologists to elucidate. There is little about it to evoke a generous enthusiasm. It lacks heroic qualities. The singularly loathsome song which celebrated the sinking of the Lusitania is as remote in spirit from such brave verse as "Admirals All," as those old sea-dogs were remote in spirit from the foul work of Von Tirpitz. No flight of fancy can conceive of Nelson counting up the women and children he had drowned. And because the whole wretched business sickened as well as affronted us, we hailed with unutterable relief any modification of its violence. For the first time in many months our souls were lightened of their load. We felt calm enough to review the summer of suspense, and to ask ourselves sincerely and soberly what were the lessons that it had taught us.

The agitation produced in this country by a terrible — and to us unexpected — European war was intensified in the spring of 1915 by the discovery that we were not so immune as we thought ourselves. It dawned slowly on men's minds that the sacrifice of the nation's honour might not after all secure the nation's safety; and this disagreeable doubt impelled us to the still more disagreeable consideration of our inadequate coast defences. Then and then only were we made aware of the chaotic confusion which reigned in the minds of our vast and unassimilated population. Then and then only did we understand that perils from without — remote and ascertainable — were brought close and rendered hid-

Counter-Currents

eously obscure by shameful coöperation from within.

Ten years ago, two years ago, we should have laughed to scorn the suggestion that any body of American citizens — no matter what their lineage — would be disloyal to the State. A belief in the integrity of citizenship was the first article of our faith. To-day, the German-American openly disavows all pretence of loyalty, and says as plainly and as publicly as he can that he will be betrayed into no conflict with his " mother country," unless the United States be actually invaded, — by which time the rest of us would feel ourselves a trifle insecure. It is strange that the men who, had they remained in their mother country (a choice which was always open to them), would never have ventured a protest against Germany's aggressive warfare, should here be so stoutly contumacious. What would have happened to the president of the New York State German-

Waiting

American Alliance, had he lived in Berlin instead of in Brooklyn, and had he spoken of the Kaiser as he dared to speak of Mr. Wilson! The license which the German (muzzled tightly in Germany) permits himself in the United States, is not unlike the license which the newly emancipated slaves in the South mistook for liberty when the Civil War was ended. It takes as many generations to make a freeman as it does to make a gentleman.

The inevitable result of this outspoken disloyalty at home was a determined and very hurtful pressure from abroad. A big, careless, self-confident nation is an easy prey; and while we waited, not very watchfully, Germany seized many chances to hit us below the belt, and hit us hard. The fomenting of strikes and labour agitation; the threatening of German workmen employed in American factories; the misuse of the radio service at Sayville, and the continued sending of code mes sages; the affidavits of Gustav Stahl before the Federal Grand Jury, and his assisted flight from the authorities; the forged American passports with which German spies wander over England and the Continent; the diplomatic indiscretions — to put it mildly — of German and Austrian ambassadors; the mysterious activities of German officials, which we were too inexperienced to understand; — all these things filled us with anger and alarm. We could not resort to the simple measures of Italians, who in Philadelphia stoned the agents whom they found trying to hold back reservists about to sail for Italy. We bore each fresh affront as though inured to provocation; but we bore it understandingly, and with deep resentment. If ever our temper snaps beneath the strain, the anger so slow to ignite will be equally hard to extinguish.

Playing consciously or unconsciously into the hands of Germany are the pac-

Waiting

ifists, — a compact body of men and women, visibly strengthened by months of indecision. Their methods may at times be laughable, but we cannot afford to laugh. I do not class under this head any of the so-called " Neutrality Leagues," and " National Peace Councils," which aim at securing a German victory by withholding munitions from the Allies. Such " neutrals " are all partisans parading under a borrowed name, which they have rendered meaningless. They have a great deal of money to spend on advertisements, and posters, and mass meetings. They can any day, in any town, fill a hall with German sympathizers who are all of one mind concerning the duty of noncombatants. Their leaders are well aware that law and usage permit, and have long permitted, to neutral nations the sale of munitions to belligerents. Their followers for the most part know this too. But it seems worth while to profess ignorance. Something can always be accomplished by agitation, were it only a murderous attack on a financier, or the smuggling of dynamite into the hold of a cargo boat.

But in reckoning up our perils, it is the fanatic, not the hypocrite, who must be taken into account. Sincerity is a terrible weapon in the hands of the ill-advised. There can be no contagion of folly, unless that folly be sincere. And what gives the uncompromising, because uncomprehending, pacifist his dangerous force is the fact that he is psychologically as inevitable as were the Iconoclasts, or the Thebaid anchorites, or any other historic instance of recoil. He is the abnormal product of abnormal conditions. The fury of war has bred this child of peace. The fumes of battle have stupefied him. Aggression and defence, brutality and heroism, the might of conquest and the right of resistance, have for him no separate significance. He is one who cannot master — as every sane man must

Waiting

learn to master — the deadly sickness of his soul.

To call the pacifist a coward is simple, but not enlightening. Cowardice is a natural and pervasive attribute of humanity. Few of us can flatly disavow it. There are women opposed to all war because their sons might be shot. A popular song — now employed to raise the spirits of school-children — expresses this sentiment. There are men opposed to all war because they might themselves be shot. So far, no music-hall ditty has exalted them. But this normal human cowardice is not infectious, save in the heat of battle, where, happily, it is seldom displayed. Infectious pacificism is a revolt from war, irrespective of abstract considerations like justice or injustice, and of personal considerations like loss or gain.

History is full of similar revolts, and they have always overstepped the limits of sanity. Because the pagan sensualist tended his body with loathsome solicitude, the Christian ascetic subjected his to loathsome indignities. The excesses of the Roman baths sanctified the uncleanliness of the early monasteries. Just as inevitable is the reaction from a ravenous war to non-resistance. Because Germany's armaments are powerful enough to terrorize Europe, we are bidden to weaken our defences. Because France and Belgium have been attacked and devastated, we are implored to take no steps for self-protection. The appeal sent out by Quaker citizens of Philadelphia — good men, ready, no doubt, to die as honourably as they have lived — was at once a confession of faith and a denial of duty. They asked that the money of the taxpayer should be spent in making "more homes happy," and they were content to leave the security of these happy homes to the unassisted care of Providence. To keep our powder dry implied mistrust of God.

Waiting

That the authorities of Iowa should strip the American flag of a white border, neatly stitched around it by the pacifists of Fort Dodge, was perhaps to be expected. The action seems peremptory; but if every society were permitted to trim and patch our national emblem, we should soon have as many flags as we have disputants in the field. For months the patient post-office officials passed on without a murmur envelopes ornamented with huge stamps, bearing pictures of a cannon partly metamorphosed into a ploughshare, a bloated child, and a pouncing dove; and inscribed with these soul-subduing lines:—

> " I am in favour of world-wide peace,
> Spread this idea, and war will cease."

The decoration of envelopes with strange devices has long afforded a vent for pent-up feelings. The peace-stamp was nobly seconded by the "peace-pin," a white enamelled dove, carrying the

Counter-Currents

motto, "World-Peace," and destined —
so its wearers assured us — to prove
itself "one of the greatest factors in
eliminating prejudices and division
lines."

Are these puerilities unworthy of consideration and comment? They are not
so preposterous as was Mr. Wanamaker's
suggestion that we should recompense
Germany for the trouble and expense she
had incurred in seizing Belgium by paying her $100,000,000,000 for her spoils.
They are not so demoralizing as the
teaching of American school-children to
calculate how many bicycles they could
buy for the money spent on the battle-
ship Oregon, or how many tickets for a
ball-game could be provided at the price
of the American navy. The Carnegie
Endowment for International Peace is to
be congratulated on having devised a
scheme by which boys and girls can be
taught arithmetically to place pleasure
above patriotism. If Germans teach their

Waiting

children to deny themselves some portion
of their mid-day meal for the needs of
Germany, and Americans teach their
children to hold ball-games and bicycles
more sacred than the needs of America,
what chance have the men we rear
against men reared to discipline and
self-sacrifice!

When an anti-enlistment league can
be formed in a country which may possibly be called to war, and anti-enlistment pledges can be signed by young
men who promise never to enroll themselves for their nation's defence, we have
cause for apprehension. When college
students can be found petitioning for
peace at any price, we have cause for
wonder. When women who have suffered nothing fling scorn at men who
have suffered all things, we have cause
in plenty for resentment.

Cause, too, for sorrow that such evil
words should be so lightly spoken. It
was but a dreary laugh that was provoked

Counter-Currents

by Miss Addams's picture of intoxicated régiments bayoneting one another under the stimulating influence of drink. Laughter is hard to come by in these dark days; but Heaven knows we should gladly have foregone the mirth to have been spared a slander so unworthy. The snatching of honour from the soldier in the hour of his utmost trial is possible only to the pacifist, who, sick with pity for pain, has lost all understanding of the things which ennoble pain: of fidelity, and courage, and the love of one's country, which, next to the love of God, is the purest of all emotions which winnow the souls of men.

The mad turmoil of folly and disaffection was kept at high pressure by the adroitness of the Imperial Government in juggling with technicalities. While we fed, like Hamlet, on the chameleon's dish, and, "promise-crammed," debated windily over words, ship after ship was sunk, and fresh exonerations and pledges were served up for our entertainment. It became difficult even for German-Americans to know just where they stood, and how far they might fittingly express their contempt for the United States, without out-distancing the Fatherland. When the " Friends of Peace" in Chicago cheered the sinking of the Hesperian, — an exploit naturally gratifying to peaceful souls, — they were silenced by more prudent members of the convention, who bethought themselves that this illustration of good faith might in turn be politely regretted. All that was left for these enthusiasts was to praise Germany's "magnanimity," to brag of her "historic friendship" for America (apparently under the impression that Lafayette was a Prussian officer), to regret the "hysteria" of Americans over the drowning of their countrymen, and to ascribe the whole war to the machinations of " Grey and Asquith, and Delcassé, and Poincaré,"

Counter-Currents

— "demons whom we should hiss and howl into the abyss of Hell."

There was plenty of disaffection in 1776, plenty in 1861 ; but we fought our two great wars without dishonour. If the Germans, well aware of our unpreparedness and of our internal dissensions, have flouted us unsparingly, it is because they are, as they have always been, densely incapable of reading the souls of men. Let us not add to our own peril by misreading the soul of Germany. We lack her discipline, we lack her unity, we lack her efficiency, the splendid result of thirty years' devotion to a single purpose. It avails us very little to analyze the "falling sickness" which has made her so mighty. Dr. Lightner Witmer, in a profoundly thoughtful and dispassionate paper on "The Relation of Intelligence to Efficiency," diagnoses her disease as "primitivism," — "meaning thereby a reversion in manners, customs, and principles to what is charac-

Waiting

teristic of a lower level of civilization."
Mr. Owen Wister, who is as poignantly
eloquent as Dr. Witmer is logical and
chill, reaches in "The Pentecost of Calamity" a somewhat similar conclusion.
"The case of Germany is a hospital
case, a case for the alienist; the mania
of grandeur complemented by the mania
of persecution." Even Mr. Bryan (always
a past-master of infelicitous argument)
tells us that a war with Germany is impossible, because it would be like "chal-
lenging an insane asylum;" — as if an
insane asylum which failed to restrain
its inmates could be left unchallenged
by the world.

It is unwise to minimize our danger
on the score of our saner judgment or
higher morality. These qualities may
win out in the future, but we are living
now. Germany is none the less terrible
because she is obsessed, and we are not
a whit safer because we recognize her obsession. The German war-maps of Paris,

Counter-Currents

cut into sections and directing which
sections were to be burned, are grim
warnings to the world. It is disturbing
to think how insensitive Paris was to
her peril when those maps were prepared. It is disturbing to think that a
fool's paradise is always the most popular playground of humanity. In the
"Atlantic Monthly" for August, 1915, an
Englishman explained lucidly to American readers (the only audience patient
enough to hear him) that non-resistance
is the road to security. Mr. Russell, "a
mathematician and a philosopher," is
confident that if England would submit
passively to invasion, and refuse passively to obey the invader, she would
suffer no great wrong. Had he read
"Sandford and Merton" when he was a
little boy, it might possibly occur to him
that Germany would treat the non-re-
sisting strikers as Mr. Barlow treated
Tommy, when that misguided child refused to dig and hoe. Had he read the

Waiting

" Bryce report," — which is not pleasant reading, — he might feel less sure that English homes and English women would be safe from assault because they lacked protectors.

The same happy confidence in our receptivity and in our limitless good nature was shown by Professor Kraus, who, in the " Atlantic Monthly " for September, 1915, conveyed to us in the plainest possible language his unfavourable opinion of the Monroe Doctrine and of its supporters. No German could be less " nice " in concealing his contempt than was this ingenuous contributor; and nothing could be better for us than to hear such words spoken at such a time. The threat of a " general accounting" was not even presented suavely to our ears, but it left us no room for doubt.

That two such arguments from two such sources should have enlivened our term of waiting is worthy of note. The

Counter-Currents

Englishman, seeing us beset by irrationalities, added one more phantasy to our load. The German, seeing us beset by alarms, added one more menace to affright us. Our patience is impervious to folly and to intimidation. We have plenty of both at home. Only an American can understand the cumulative anger in his countryman's heart as affront is added to affront, and the slow lapse of time brings us neither redress nor redemption. However sanguine and however peace-loving we may be, we cannot well base our hopes of future security on the tenderness shown us in the past. If long months of painful suspense, of hope alternating with despondency, and pride with shame, have wrought no other good, they have at least revealed to us where our danger lies. They have bared disloyalty, and have put good citizens on their guard.

Somewhere in the mind of the nation is a saving sanity. Somewhere in the

Waiting

heart of the nation is a saving grace. A day may come when these two harmonious qualities will find expression in the simple words of Cardinal Newman: "The best prudence is to have no fear."

Americanism

WHENEVER we stand in need of intricate knowledge, balanced judgment, or delicate analysis, it is our comfortable habit to question our neighbours. They may be no wiser and no better informed than we are; but a collective opinion has its value, or at least its satisfying qualities. For one thing, there is so much of it. For another, it seldom lacks variety. Two years ago the "American Journal of Sociology" asked two hundred and fifty "representative" men and women " upon what ideals, policies, programmes, or specific purposes should Americans place most stress in the immediate future," and published the answers that were returned in a Symposium entitled, "What is Americanism?" The candid reader, following this symposium, received much counsel, but little

Americanism

enlightenment. There were some good practical suggestions; but nowhere any cohesion, nowhere any sense of solidarity, nowhere any concern for national honour or authority.

It was perhaps to be expected that Mr. Burghardt Du Bois's conception of true Americanism would be the abolishment of the colour line, and that Mr. Eugene Debs would see salvation in the sweeping away of "privately owned industries, and production for individual profit." These answers might have been foreseen when the questions were asked. But it was disconcerting to find that all, or almost all, of the "representative" citizens represented one line of civic policy, or civic reform, and refused to look beyond it. The prohibitionist discerned Americanism in prohibition, the equal suffragist in votes for women, the biologist in applied science, the physician in the extirpation of microbes, the philanthropist in playgrounds, the sociologist

261

in eugenism and old-age pensions, and the manufacturer in the revision of taxes. It was refreshing when an author unexpectedly demanded the extinction of inherited capital. Authorship seldom concerns itself with anything so inconceivably remote.

The quality of miscellaneousness is least serviceable when we leave the world of affairs, and seek admission into the world of ideals. There must be an interpretation of Americanism which will express for all of us a patriotism at once practical and emotional, an understanding of our place in the world, and of the work we are best fitted to do in it, a sentiment which we can hold — as we hold nothing else — in common, and which will be forever remote from personal solicitude and resentment. Those of us whose memories stretch back over half a century recall too plainly a certain uneasiness which for years pervaded American politics and American letters, which made

Americanism

us unduly apprehensive, and, as a consequence, unduly sensitive and arrogant. It found expression in Mr. William Cullen Bryant's well-known poem, "America," made familiar to my generation by school readers and manuals of elocution, and impressed by frequent recitations upon our memories.

"O mother of a mighty race,
Yet lovely in thy youthful grace!
The elder dames, thy haughty peers,
Admire and hate thy blooming years;
With words of shame
And taunts of scorn they join thy name."

There are eight verses, and four of them repeat Mr. Bryant's conviction that the nations of Europe united in envying and insulting us. To be hated because we were young, and strong, and good, and beautiful, seemed, to my childish heart, a noble fate; and when a closer acquaintance with history dispelled this pleasant illusion, I parted from it with regret. France was our ally in the Revolutionary War. Russia was friendly in the Civil War. England was friendly in the Spanish War. If the repudiation of state debts left a bad taste in the mouths of foreign investors, they might be pardoned for making a wry face. Most of them were subsequently paid; but the phrase "American revoke" dates from the period of suspense. By the time we celebrated our hundredth birthday with a world's fair, we were on very easy terms with our neighbours. Far from taunting us with shameful words, our "haughty peers" showed on this memorable occasion unanimous good temper and good will; and " Punch's " congratulatory verses were among the most pleasant birthday letters we received.

The expansion of national life, fed by the great emotions of the Civil War, and revealed to the world by the Centennial Exhibition, found expression in education, art, and letters. Then it was that Americanism took a new and disconcerting turn. Pleased with our progress, stunned by finding that we had poets, and painters, and novelists, and magazines, and a history, all of our own, we began to say, and say very loudly, that we had no need of the poets, and painters, and novelists, and magazines, and histories of other lands. Our attitude was not unlike that of George Borrow, who, annoyed by the potency of Italian art, adjured Englishmen to stay at home and contemplate the greatness of England. England, he said, had pictures of her own. She had her own "minstrel strain." She had all her sons could ask for. "England against the world."

In the same exclusive spirit, American school boards proposed that American school-children should begin the study of history with the colonization of America, ignoring the trivial episodes which preceded this great event. Patriotic protectionists heaped duties on foreign art, and bade us buy American pictures. En-

Counter-Currents

thusiastic editors confided to us that "the world has never known such storehouses of well-selected mental food as are furnished by our American magazines." Complacent critics rejoiced that American poets did not sing like Tennyson, "nor like Keats, nor Shelley, nor Wordsworth"; but that, as became a new race of men, they "reverberated a synthesis of all the poetic minds of the century." Finally, American novelists assured us that in their hands the art of fiction had grown so fine and rare that we could no longer stand the "mannerisms" of Dickens, or the "confidential attitude" of Thackeray. We had scaled the empyrean heights.

There is a brief paragraph in Mr. Thayer's "Life and Letters of John Hay," which vividly recalls this peculiar phase of Americanism. Mr. Hay writes to Mr. Howells in 1882: "The worst thing in our time about American taste is the way it treats James. I believe he would not be

Americanism

read in America at all if it were not for his European vogue. If he lived in Cambridge, he could write what he likes; but because he finds London more agreeable, he is the prey of all the patriotisms. Of all vices, I hold patriotism the worst, when it meddles with matters of taste."

So far had American patriotism encroached upon matters of taste, that by 1892 there was a critical embargo placed upon foreign literature. "Every nation," we were told, "ought to supply its own second-rate books," — like domestic sheeting and ginghams. An acquaintance with English authors was held to be a misdemeanour. Why quote Mr. Matthew Arnold, when you might quote Mr. Lowell? Why write about Becky Sharp, when you might write about Hester Prynne? Why laugh over Dickens, when you might laugh over Mark Twain? Why eat artichokes, when you might eat corn? American school-boys, we were told, must be guarded from the feudalism of Scott. American speech must be guarded from the "insularities" of England's English. "That failure in good sense which comes from too warm a self-satisfaction" (Mr. Arnold does sometimes say a thing very well) robbed us for years of mental poise, of adjusted standards, of an unencumbered outlook upon life.

It is strange to glance back upon a day when we had so little to trouble us that we could vex our souls over feudalism and fiction ; when — in the absence of serious problems — we could raise pronunciation or spelling into a national issue. Americanism has done with trivialities, patriotism with matters of taste. Love for one's country is not a shallow sentiment, based upon self-esteem. It is a profound and primitive passion. It may lie dormant in our souls when all goes well. It may be thwarted and frustrated by the exigencies of party government. It may be dissevered from pride or pleas-

Americanism

ure. But it is part of ourselves, wholly beyond analysis, fed upon hope and fear, joy and sorrow, glory and shame. If, after the fashion of the world, we drowsed in our day of security, we have been rudely and permanently awakened. The shadow of mighty events has fallen across our path. We have witnessed a great national crime. We have beheld the utmost heights of heroism. And when we asked of what concern to us were this crime and this heroism, the answer came unexpectedly, and with blinding force. The sea was strewn with our dead, our honour was undermined by conspiracies, our factories were fired, our cargoes dynamited. We were a neutral nation at peace with the world. The attack made upon our industries and upon our good name was secret, malignant, and pitiless. It was organized warfare, without the courage and candour of war.

The unavowed enemy who strikes in the dark is hard to reach, but he is outside the pale of charity. There was something in the cold fury of Mr. Wilson's words, when, in his message to Congress, he denounced the traitors " who have poured the poison of disloyalty into the very arteries of our national life," which turned that unexpansive state-paper into a human document, and drove it straight to the human hearts of an injured and insulted people. Under the menace of disloyalty, Americanism has taken new form and substance; and our just resentment, like the potter's wheel, has moulded this force into lines of strength and resistance. We have seen all we want to see of "frightfulness" in Europe, all we want to see of injustice, supported by violence. We are not prepared to welcome any scheme of terrorization in the interests of a foreign power, or any interference of a foreign power with our legitimate fields of industry. Such schemes and such interference constitute an inconceivable affront to the nation.

Americanism

Their stern and open disavowal is the shibboleth by which our elections may be purged of treachery, and our well-being confided to good citizenship.

Of all the countries in the world, we and we only have any need to create artificially the patriotism which is the birthright of other nations. Into the hearts of six millions of foreign-born men — less than half of them naturalized — we must infuse that quality of devotion which will make them place the good of the state above their personal good, and the safety of the state above their personal safety. It is like pumping oxygen into six million pairs of lungs for which the common air is not sufficiently stimulating. We must also keep a watchful eye upon these men's wives, — when they are so blessed, — and concentrate our supreme energy on uncounted milions of children, whose first step toward patriotism is the acquirement of a common tongue.

Counter-Currents

We are trying fitfully, but in good faith, to work this civic miracle. Americanization Day is but one expression of the nation-wide endeavour. When Cleveland invited all her citizens who had been naturalized within a twelvemonth to assemble and receive a public welcome, to sit on a platform and be made much of, to listen to national songs and patriotic speeches, and to take home, every man, a flag and a seal of the city, she set a good example which will be widely followed. The celebrations at Riverside, California, and New York City's Pageant of the Nations had in view the same admirable end. Sentiment is not a substitute for duty and discipline ; but it has its uses and its field of efficacy. Such ceremonies perseveringly repeated for twenty years might work a change in the immigrant population of to-day, were we secure from the fresh millions which threaten us to-morrow. That the Fourth of July

Americanism

should be often selected for these rites
is perhaps inevitable; it is a time when
patriotism assumes a vivid and popular
aspect; but Heaven forbid that we should
rechristen Independence Day, Americanization Day! However ready we may
be to welcome our new citizens, however confident we may be of their value
to the Republic, we are not yet prepared
to give them the place of honour hitherto held by the signers of the Declaration of Independence. The name which
perpetuates the memory of that deed
is a sacred name, and should be preserved no less sacredly than the national life which was then committed to
our keeping.

It is no insult to the immigrant to say
that he constitutes one of the perils of
Americanism. How can it be otherwise?
Assume that he is a law-abiding citizen,
that he knows nothing of the conspiracies which have imperilled our safety,
that he does not propose to use his vote

Counter-Currents

in the interests of a foreign power, and that the field of hyphenated politics has no existence for him. For all these boons we are sufficiently grateful. But how far does he understand the responsibilities he assumes with the franchise, how far does he realize that he has become part of the machinery of the state, and how far can we depend upon him in our hour of need? He knows, or at least he has been told, that he may not return home to fight for his own country, if he seeks American citizenship. He must resist a natural and a noble impulse as the price of his coveted "papers." But will there spring in his heart a noble, though not very natural, impulse to fight for us if we call our sons to arms? Can we hope that his native intelligence, unshackled by any working knowledge of our language, will grasp our national policy and our national obligations ; and that — free from conscription — he will voluntarily risk his life in behalf of a government for which he has no inheritance of fidelity?

We have opened our doors to unrestricted immigration, partly because capitalists want plenty of cheap labour, which is not a good reason; and partly because the immigrants want to come, which is not a sufficient reason. They also — despite the heart-rending conditions depicted by Miss Frances Kellor — want to stay. Those who return to the higher standards of Europe do not materially affect the situation. They stay, and either surmount their difficulties, or, succumbing to them, fill our asylums, hospitals, and almshouses. For many years, foreign economists must have looked with relief at the countless thousands of derelicts who were supported by the United States instead of by their own governments. But even the satisfaction we have thus afforded does not wholly justify our course. Is it worth our while to fill the air with clamour over eugenics

Counter-Currents

and birth-control, to build barriers around a marriage license, and to dramatize impassioned pleas for sterility, when the birthrate of the Republic is nobody's concern? If the survival of the fittest means as much to the commonwealth as to the family, why should we fiddle over pathology while the nation burns?

Miss Kellor is not the only kind-hearted American who holds her countrymen to blame for the deficiencies of the immigrant. Her point of view is a common one, and has some foundation in fact. She censures us even for his dirt, though if she had ever listened to the vitriolic comments of the police, she might revise her judgment on that score. "Can't you *do* anything?" I once asked a disconsolate guardian of the peace, who stood on a fine hot day contemplating the forth-flung garbage of the Israelite. To which he made answer: "Did ye iver thry to clane out a sthable wid a toothpick?" And as this had not been one of

Americanism

my life's endeavours, I offered no further comment. But Miss Kellor touches a vital truth when she says that Americans will never weld a mass of heterogeneous humanity into a nation, until they are able to say what they want that nation to be, and until they are prepared to follow a policy intelligently outlined. In other words, Americanism is not a medley of individual theories, partial philanthropies, and fluid sentiment. A consistent nationalism is essential to civic life, and we are not dispensed from achieving consistent nationalism by the difficulties in our way. No multiplication of difficulties makes an impossibility. Upon what props did the Venetians build the fairest city of the world?

We cannot in this country hope for the compelling devotion which has animated Germany; still less for the supreme moral and intellectual force which is the staying power of France. Mrs. Wharton has best described the intelli-

gence with which Frenchmen translate
their ideals into doctrine. They know for
what they stand in the civilized world,
and the first " white heat of dedication "
has hardened into steel-like endurance.
To the simple emotions of men who are
defending their homes from assault have
been added the emotions of men who
are defending the world's noblest inheritance from degradation. " It is the rea-
soned recognition of this peril which is
making the most intelligent people in
the world the most sublime."

The problems of England are so closely
akin to our own problems, and her perplexities are so closely akin to our own
perplexities, that we should regard them
with insight and with sympathy. We too
must pause in every keen emergency to
cajole, to persuade, to placate, to reconcile conflicting interests, to humour conflicting opinions, — termed by those who
hold them, "principles." We too must
forever bear in mind the political party

Americanism

which is in power, and the political party which waits to get into power; and we must pick our way as best we can by the cross-lights of their abiding hostility. We too must face and overcome the dough-like resistance of apathy.

I have been told — though I refuse to believe it on hearsay— that British labourers have asked what difference it would make to them whether they worked for British or for German masters. It is quite true that British pacifists and British radicals have not only put this question, but have answered it, greatly to their own satisfaction, in American periodicals; but American periodicals; are not mouthpieces of the British workmen. I make no doubt that if we were fighting for our lives, there would be found American pacifists and American radicals writing in British periodicals that no great harm would come to America if she submitted passively to invasion ; and that, whether their country's cause were right or wrong,

the slaughter of her sons was a crime,
and the wealth of her capitalists was a
sufficient reason for refusing to do battle
for her liberty. The painful certainty that
we should never be free from the bab-
bling of treason, any more than England
is free from it now, makes Americanism
(the Americanism which means civic loyalty founded on civic intelligence) shine
like a far-off star on a very dim horizon.

At present, disloyalty founded upon
ignorance meets with more attention
than it deserves. Why, after all, should
two thousand people assemble in New
York to hear Miss Helen Keller say that,
in the event of invasion, the American
workman "has nothing to lose but his
chains"? He has his manhood to lose, and
it should mean as much to him as to any
millionaire in the land. What new and
debilitating doctrine is this which holds
that personal honour is the exclusive attribute of wealth, and that a labourer
has no more business with it than has a

Americanism

dog! The fact that Miss Keller has overcome the heavy disabilities which nature
placed in her path, lends interest to her person, but no weight to her opinions, which
give evidence of having been adopted
wholesale, and of having never filtered
through any reasoning process of her
own. It is always agreeable to hear her
speak about good and simple things.
When she said in Philadelphia that happiness does not lie in pleasure, and that,
although she did not expect to be always pleased, she did expect to be always
happy, by doing what she could to make
those about her happy, we gave our
hearty concurrence to sentiments so un-
exceptionable. It was the way we ourselves should have liked to feel, and we
knew it was our own fault that we did
not. But when in New York she adjured
workingmen never to enter the United
States Army, and informed us that all
we needed for adequate defence were
shooting-galleries "within reach of every

family," so that we could all learn — like the old ladies in "Punch" — to fire a gun, there was something profoundly sad in words so ill-judged and so fatuous. It cannot be a matter of no moment that, in the hour of our danger and indecision, thousands of people stand ready to applaud the disloyal utterances which should affront every honourable man or woman who hears them.

The "Yale Review" quotes the remark of a "foreigner" that Americans are always saying, "I don't care." The phrase is popular, and sounds disheartening ; but if we spare ourselves concern over trivial things (if, for example, we were not excited or inflamed by Captain von Papen's calling us "idiotic Yankees "), it does not follow that big issues leave us unmoved. If they did, if they ever should, the word Americanism might as well be obliterated from the language. The consistent nationalism for which it stands admits of no indifference. It is true that the possible peril of New York — as defenceless as a soft-shell crab, and as succulent — is not an ever-present care to San Francisco. It is true that San Francisco's deep anxiety over Japanese immigration and land-ownership was lightly treated by New York. And it is true that Denver, sitting in the safety zone, looks down from her lofty heights without any pressing solicitude about either of her sister cities. But just as the San Francisco earthquake wrung the heart of New York, so the first gun fired at New York would arm the citizens of San Francisco. Only it might then be too late.

The Christmas cartoon of Uncle Sam holding a package marked "Peace and Prosperity," and saying with a broad smile, "Just what I wanted!" was complacent rather than comprehensive. We want peace and we want prosperity, but they are not all we want; partly because their permanency depends upon certain props which seem to many of us a bit unsteady, and partly because we do not, any more than other men, live by bread alone. The things of the spirit are for us, even as for heroic and suffering France, of vital worth and import. If we could say with certainty, "All is gained but honour," there are still some of us who would feel our blessings incomplete; but, as it chances, the contempt meted out to us has taken the palpable form of encroachment upon our common rights. Until we can protect our industries from assault and our citizens from butchery, until we can couple disavowal of past injuries with real assurance of safety in the future, peace limps, and prosperity is shadowed. With every fresh shock we have received, with every fresh sorrow we have endured, there has come to us more and more clearly the vision of a noble nationalism, purged of "comfort-mongering," and of perverted sentiment.

Cynical newspaper writers have be-

Americanism

gun to say that the best way to make Americans forget one injury is to inflict on them another. This is hardly a half-truth. The sinking of the Ancona did not obliterate from our minds the names of the Falaba, the Gulflight, the Frye, the Hesperian, the Arabic, and the Lusitania. Neither has the sinking of the Persia buried the Ancona in oblivion. And it is not simple humanity which has burned these names into the tablets of our memories. The loss of American lives through the savage torpedoing of liners and merchant ships might be doubled and trebled any summer day by the sinking of an excursion steamer, and we should soon forget. A country which reports eight thousand murders in a single year is not wont to be deeply stirred by the perils which beset our munition-workers. But when Americans have gone to their deaths through the violence of another government, or in the interests of another government, then the

Counter-Currents

wrong done them is elevated to the importance of a national calamity, and redress becomes a national obligation. Because we do not wearily reiterate this patent truth does not mean that we have forgotten it. If words could save, if words could heal, we should have no fear, nor shame, nor sorrow. Nothing is less worth while than to go on prattling about a consistent foreign policy. The cornerstone of civilization is man's dependence for protection on the state which he has reared for his own safety and support.

The concern of Americans for America (I use the word to symbolize the United States) must be the deep and loyal sentiment which brooks no injustice and no insult. We have need of many things, but first and foremost of fidelity. It is a matter of pride and pleasure that some of our foreign-born citizens should excel in art and letters; that, under our tutelage, they should learn to design posters, model statuary, write poems, and

Americanism

make speeches. These things have their admitted place and value. The encouragement which is given them, the opportunities which are made for them, the praise which is lavished upon them, are proofs of our good-will, and of our genuine delight in fostering ability. But the real significance of the "Americanization" movement, the summoning of conferences, the promoting of exhibitions, the bestowing of prizes, is the need we all feel of unification, the hope we all cherish that, through the influence of congenial work, immigrants and the children of immigrants will become one in spirit with the native born. We could make shift to do without the posters and the symbolic statuary; we could read fewer poems and listen to fewer speeches ; but we cannot possibly do without the loyalty which we have a right to demand, and which is needful to the safety of the Republic.

For the main thing to be borne in

mind is that Americanization does not mean only an increase of opportunity for the alien, an effort toward his permanent well-being. It means also service and sacrifice on his part. This is what citizenship entails, although voters and those who clamour for the vote seldom take into account such an inexorable truth. The process of assimilation must go deeper than the polling booth and the trade union can carry it. Democracy forever teases us with the contrast between its ideals and its realities, between its heroic possibilities and its sorry achievements. But it is our appointed road, and the stones over which we perpetually stumble deny us the drowsy perils of content. When we read Dr. Eliot's noble words in praise of free government and equal opportunities, we know that his amazing buoyancy does not imply ignorance of primaries, of party methods, and of graft. With these things he has been familiar all his life ; but the creaking ma-

Americanism

chinery of democracy has never dimmed his faith in its holiness. Remediable disorders, however grievous and deep-seated, afford us the comfort of hope, and the privilege of unending exertion.

To no one ignorant of history can the right of citizenship assume any real significance. In our country the ballot is so carelessly guarded, so shamefully misused, that it has become to some men a subject of derision; to many, an unconsidered trifle; to all, or almost all, an expression of personal opinion, which, at its best, reflects a popular newspaper, and, at its worst, stands for nothing less hurtful than stupidity. A recent contributor to the "Unpopular Review" reminds us soberly that, as the democratic state cannot rise above the level of its voters, and as nationality means for us merely the will of the people, it might not be amiss to guard the franchise with reasonable solicitude, and to ask something more than unlimited ignorance, and the

Counter-Currents

absence of a criminal record, as its price. If every man — alien or native-born — who casts his ballot could be made to know and to feel that "all the political forces of his country were mainly occupied for a hundred years in making that act possible," and that the United States is, and has always been, the nation of those "who willed to be Americans," citizenship might become for us what it was to Rome, what it is to France, — the exponent of honour, the symbol of self-sacrifice.

A knowledge of history might also prove serviceable in enabling us to recognize our place and our responsibility among the nations of the world. No remoteness (geographical remoteness counts for little in the twentieth century) can sever our interests from the interests of Europe, or lift from our shoulders the burden of helping to sustain the collective rights of mankind. We know now that the menace of frightfulness has

Americanism

overshadowed us. We know that, however cautiously we picked our steps, we could not, and did not, escape molestation. But even if we had saved our own skin, if we had suffered no destruction of property, and if none of our dead lay under the water, the freedom of Europe, the future of democracy, and the rights of man would be to us matters of concern.

It is true, moreover, that friendship and alliance with those European states whose aspirations and ideals respond to our own aspirations and ideals, are as consistent with Americanism as are friendship and alliance with the states of South America, which we are now engaged in loving. It is not from Bolivia, or Chile, or Venezuela, or the Argentine that we have drawn our best traditions, our law, language, literature, and art. We extend to these "sister Republics" the arms of commercial affection; but they have no magic words like Magna

Counter-Currents

Charta and *le Tiers État* to stir our souls an inch beyond self-profit. When we count up our assets, we must reckon heavily on the respect of those nations which we most respect, and whose good-will in the past is a guarantee of good-will in the future. It is worth our while, even from the standpoint of American-ism, to prove our fellowship with hu-manity, our care for other interests than our own. The civilization of the world is the business of all who live in the world. We cannot see it crashing down, as it crashed in the sinking of the Lusitania and the Ancona, and content ourselves with asking how many Americans were drowned. Noble standards, and noble sympathies, and noble sorrows have their driving power, their practical util-ity. They have counted heavily in the destinies of nations. Carthage had com-merce. Rome had ideals.

THE END